Mirror (a.k.a. *Zerkalo* or *The Bright, Bright Day*) is Andrei Tarkovsky's beloved project. It remained his favourite film, and closest to his concept of cinema.

Mirror (1975) is loosely autobiographical, and combines many elements, ranging from poetry read in voiceover by the director's father, to dream sequences, flashbacks, newsreel and memory devices. The movie is a poetic exploration of childhood. Film as personal psychogeography, self-reflexive, even indulgent.

This pocket movie guide includes a scene-by-scene brekadown of *Mirror*, and a survey of the critical reception of the production.

Mirror

Andrei Tarkovsky

Pocket Movie Guide

Andrei Tarkovsky
Mirror
Pocket Guide

Jeremy Mark Robinson

CRESCENT MOON

CRESCENT MOON PUBLISHING
P.O. Box 1312, Maidstone, Kent, ME14 5XU
Great Britain, www.crmoon.com

First published 2024.
© Jeremy Mark Robinson 2024.

Set in Times New Roman 9 on 12pt.
Designed by Radiance Graphics.

The right of Jeremy Mark Robinson to be identified as the author of *Andrei Tarkovsky: Mirror* has been asserted generally in accordance with sections 77 and 78 of the Copyright, Designs and Patents Act 1988.

All rights reserved. No part of this book may be reprinted or reproduced, stored in a retrieval system, or transmitted, in any form or by any means, electronic, mechanical, photocopying, recording or otherwise, without permission from the publisher.

British Library Cataloguing in Publication data available for this title.

ISBN 9781861713018

Contents

Acknowledgements • 7
Abbreviations • 8

PART ONE: ANDREI TARKOVSKY

1   Introduction • 16
2   The Poetry of Cinema • 22
3   Tarkovsky's Symbols • 33

PART TWO: *MIRROR*

4   *Mirror* • 53
5   *Mirror*: Aspects of the Production • 65
6   *Mirror*: Scene By Scene • 92
7   Critical Responses To *Mirror* • 142

Filmography • 150
Availability • 155
Bibliography • 156

Acknowledgements

Thanks to: Danny Rivers, Chris Fassnidge, Artificial Eye, British Film Institute Library, University College for the Creative Arts Library, Kent County Library, West Kent College Library.

Acknowledgements to authors quoted and their publishers: British Film Institute. Faber & Faber. Indiana University Press. Oxford University Press. Seagull Books, Calcutta. Prentice-Hall. Penguin. Thames & Hudson. *Iskusstvo kino. Sight and Sound. Positif.* McGraw-Hill. Russian Cinema Council. Routledge.

Quotes from the poetry of Arseny Tarkovsky are taken from *Life, Life: Selected Poems*, tr. V. Rounding, Crescent Moon, 1999/ 2008.

Picture credits:
Museum of Modern Art Film Stills Archive. Films Incorporated. Jerry Ohlinger's Movie Material Store. Evgeny Tsimbal. National Film Archive, London. Swedish Film Institute. Artificial Eye. Contemporary Films.

Abbreviations

ST = *Sculpting in Time*, by Andrei Tarkovsky
D = *Time Within Time: The Diaries 1970-1986*, by Andrei Tarkovsky
CS = *Collected Screenplays*, by Andrei Tarkovsky
JP = *The Films of Andrei Tarkovsky*, by Vida T. Johnson and Graham Petrie

And this I dreamt, and this I dream,
And some time this I will dream again,
And all will be repeated, all be re-embodied,
You will dream everything I have seen in dream.

To one side from ourselves, to one side from
                               the world
Wave follows wave to break on the shore,
On each wave is a star, a person, a bird,
Dreams, reality, death – on wave after wave.

Arseny Tarkovsky
(from ''And this I dreamt, and this I dream'')

We celebrated every moment
Of our meetings as epiphanies,
Just we two in all the world.
Bolder, lighter than a bird's wing,
You hurtled like vertigo
Down the stairs, leading
Through moist lilac to your realm
Beyond the mirror.

Arseny Tarkovsky, 'First Meetings'

Andrei Tarkovsky on the set of Mirror

PART ONE

ANDREI TARKOVSKY

1

INTRODUCTION

My first encounter with Andrei Tarkovsky's cinema was seeing *Mirror* (1975, a.k.a. *Zerkalo* or *The Bright, Bright Day*), when it was broadcast on British television in 1982. I was struck by the image of the trees blowing in the wind at night. This is intensely poetic – about as deeply poetic as cinema ever gets. It is one of the starting points for the film, for the childhood scenes. It is scene four: the boy is in bed; night noises are heard – a bird; cut to some trees and bushes: the camera tracks slowly, laterally, to the left; a breeze rustles the trees; cut back to the boy; he leans up in the bed and says, 'Papa'. The yearning in this sequence is immense. It's so simple (or seems so): just a shot of a boy in a bed and some trees. Yet Tarkovsky's sacred cinema manages to imbue it with such richness, such power, such mystery. One is not sure exactly how he does it. The elements appear mundane, viewed individually. One can recognize the language, the techniques, the signs and symbols, and so on, but none of this knowledge explains the mystery. Tarkovsky's art transcends ordinary cinematic approaches.

LIFE

Andrei Tarkovsky (April 4, 1932, Zavrazhye – December 29, 1986, Paris) is one of the most fascinating of filmmakers. He is supremely romantic, an old-fashioned, traditional artist – at home in the company of Leonardo da Vinci, Pieter Brueghel, Aleksandr Pushkin, Fyodor Dostoievsky, Byzantine icon painters and Romantics such as Johann Wolfgang von Goethe. Tarkovsky is a magician, no question, but argues for demystification (even while his films celebrate mystery. It's not a contradiction for him). He speaks endlessly of the 'truth', of 'spirit', of 'faith'. He talks in Christian, Platonic, Neoplatonic, Romantic, metaphysical and religious terms. He is a purist, always aiming for the essence of things. His films are full of magical events, dreams, memory sequences, multiple viewpoints, multiple time-scales and bizarre occurrences. He is a marvellous filmmaker, a creator of miracles, a 'maker', a poet (the Greek word *poeitas* means 'maker').

Few contemporary filmmakers have even a millionth of the mystery and depth of Andrei Tarkovsky's art. Tarkovsky has an extraordinary feeling for sensuous experiences. *The Sacrifice* is surely one of the most voluptuous films ever made. It has a præternatural feeling for surfaces, for texture and light and space. And yet, although Tarkovsky is a master of the presentation of surfaces – all that glass and water and polished wood and metal – his images also contain such depth. It is a depth only attained by directors such as Robert Bresson, Pier Paolo Pasolini and Werner Herzog. Tarkovsky has a deeply subtle sense of space. Contemporary Hollywood directors can create spaces very quickly and dynamically in films – with their over-determined, self-conscious use of the camera, point-of-view, motion and editing. But Hollywood's filmic spaces can appear as mainly superficial gloss, and the characters are too often cardboard cut-outs. Tarkovsky's cinema, meanwhile, achieves a sense of depth on every level: the visual, temporal, symbolic, kinetic, personal, social, narrative and spiritual.

Andrei Tarkovsky studied film at V.G.I.K. (the All-Union State Cinema Institute, formerly G.T.K. and G.I.K.), founded in 1919 by Vladimir Gardin, Lev Kuleshov and others. At V.G.I.K., Tarkovsky made a short TV film (*Segodnya uvol'neniya ne budget/ There*

Will Be No Leave Today [1959]) and his graduation diploma piece, *The Steamroller and the Violin* (1961). (Maya Turovskaya reckoned that Mikhail Romm was a significant influence on Tarkovsky's career, and many of his contemporaries too: Romm helped his students, lent them money, and defended their films against the authorities. Romm was 'the most lively and adaptable of the older generation of filmmakers', Turovskaya said [21]).

Many of the great names of Soviet cinema studied or taught at the All-Union State Cinema Institute, including: Sergei Bondarchuk, Nikolai Batalov, Alexander Dovzhenko, Mikhail Romm (one of Andrei Tarkovsky's teachers), Sergei Yutkevich, Marlen Khutsiev, Sergei Eisenstein, Vsevolod Pudovkin and Grigori Kotzintsev. At film school (V.G.I.K.), Tarkovsky saw many films as part of his course: *Citizen Kane, The Little Foxes*, Jean Renoir, Jean Vigo, John Ford, the Italian Neorealist directors, and Andrzej Wajda and Andrzej Munk (the Polish School). When Tarkovsky was offering advice to young movie-makers about which directors to study, he suggested five masters: Alexander Dovzhenko, Luis Buñuel, Ingmar Bergman, Michelangelo Antonioni and Carl-Theodor Dreyer (D, 361). At film school, students should watch lots of films, Tarkovsky recommended, and should also read lots of books (and not just the set texts).

Andrei Tarkovsky was born in Zavrazhye, near Yuryevets, on the River Volga. His early life was spent in the country, when his parents moved out of Moscow (but the Tarkovskys moved back to the city fairly soon). Tarkovsky would later poeticize his early life near Yuryevets in *Mirror*, but he spent far less time there than in Moscow. During WW2, the family moved into the countryside around Yuryevets while Arseny Tarkovsky fought in the war. Vida Johnson and Graham Petrie call the 'major trauma' of Tarkovsky's youth the break-up of the family and Tarkovsky's father being absent (JP, 18).

In his youth, Andrei Tarkovsky worked in the far East

of Russia, in the Turukhansky region and the Kureika river, making sketches and conducting research for a scientific institute. The year he spent exploring the *taiga* in Turukhansky was an important time for Tarkovsky. A lesser-known fact about Tarkovsky's career is that he worked in the mid-Sixties at the All-Soviet radio station. He directed a radio play based on a William Faulkner short story.

Andrei Tarkovsky's mother worked at the First State Publishing House in Moscow as an editor (some of that life finds its way into *Mirror*). Maria Ivanovna was a major force in inspiring Tarkovsky to become an artist; she was also 'a very strict disciplinarian' (JP, 19). Tarkovsky said that his mother 'obviously had a very strong influence on me – influence is not even the right word – simply the whole world is for me connected with my mother'.

Andrei Tarkovsky's first wife, Irma Rauch, had been his classmate at the All-Union State Cinema Institute; they wed in 1957. Tarkovsky's first son, Arseny, was born in 1962. (Commentators have noted how Tarkovsky junior followed his father in leaving his first wife and child.) As echoed in *Mirror*, Tarkovsky grew up surrounded by women. Tarkovsky found the emotional environment oppressive as well as inspiring.

Andrei Tarkovsky married Larissa Pavlovna Yegorkina, his second wife, in 1970 (they had met and romanced during the shooting of *Andrei Roublyov*). They had a son, Andrei (born in 1970). Larissa worked on Tarkovsky's films on set (she was assistant director for *Mirror*, for instance). Since Tarkovsky's death in 1986, Larissa was increasingly the guardian of Tarkovsky's flame. She helped to edit Tarkovsky's diaries, which were published in 1991 as *Time Within Time* (*Martyrlog* in Germany). Much of Tarkovsky's private life was excised from the diaries, as well as his personal comments on his contemporaries and friends.

By most accounts, Larissa Tarkovskaya was a formidable personality, and was keen to shape the Tarkovsky cult as it grew after the director's demise.

Tarkovskaya in particular fell out with Tarkovsky's sister Marina (and she often fought with Tarkovsky too).

After *Nostalghia*, Andrei Tarkovsky wasn't granted permission to continue to work outside Russia, and in 1984 he announced his decision to stay in the West. His wife, Larissa, had been allowed to join him in Europe, but not his son Andrei. While he lived in the West, Tarkovsky attended film festivals (such as Telluride), directed operas (*Boris Godunov*), and gave lectures. Tarkovsky didn't know he had cancer while he was shooting *The Sacrifice*; he was diagnosed in December, 1985, when the film had already been made.

Among Andrei Tarkovsky's regular collaborators were fellow director and scriptwriter Andrei Mikhailkov-Konchalovsky, actors Anatoly Solonitsyn, Nikolai Grinko, Nikolai Burlyaev, Erland Josephson (a Bergman regular) and Oleg Yankovsky, composers Eduard Artemiev (*Solaris, Mirror, Stalker*) and Vyacheslav Ovchinniko (*Ivan's Childhood* and *Andrei Roublyov*), set designer A. Merkulov (*Mirror, Stalker*), cameraman Vadim Yusov (*The Steamroller and the Violin, Ivan's Childhood, Andrei Roublyov, Solaris, Mirror*), costume designer Nelli Fomina (*Solaris, Mirror, Stalker*), producer Tamara Ogorodnikov (*Andrei Robulyov*; she also acted in *Mirror* and *Solaris*), and editor Lyudmilla Feiginova (*Andrei Roublyov, Solaris, Mirror, Stalker*).

AVAILABILITY

Manufacturers and distributors of Andrei Tarkovsky's films on DVD and video include the Russian Cinema Council (Ruscico), Kino Video, Artificial Eye, Fox Lober, Criterion, Image Entertainment, and Facets Video. Home DVD and video distribution have brought new problems in Tarkovsky studies – with the quality of prints, of transfers, of audio quality, of soundtracks, and 'restoration'. Issues such as the director's 'intentions', 'director's cuts', and sound remixes are confronted yet again.

The seven features are available on video and DVD in the West, though you may have to hunt around a bit to find them, even in big stores. Andrei Tarkovsky seems to have a dedicated but relatively small following. One can't imagine his films being consumed in large quantities in the home entertainment sector like mainstream films coming out of Hong Kong, Bollywood, Paris, Rome or Hollywood. On the plus side, it's not too difficult obtaining the collected works on home entertainment formats: there are only seven features and two shorts to buy (*The Steamroller and the Violin* and *There Will Be No Leave Today*). The documentary by Michal Leszczylowski about the making of *The Sacrifice* is a must-have, as is the documentary Tarkovsky made in Italy, *Tempo di Viaggio*. (Some other documentaries are also available, including one on the making of *Nostalghia*). But there are no different editions or 'director's cuts' of the films to collect (though the different versions of *Andrei Roublyov* would be great to have, but it's highly unlikely they'll appear, given Tarkovsky's relatively small sales). Some of the DVDs and videos of Tarkovsky's movies come with documentaries, some specially made (valuable interviews with, for instance, Tarkovsky's cameramen, Vadim Yusov and A. Knyazhinsky, production designer R. Safiullin, composer Vyacheslav Ovchinnikov, or actors E. Zharikov and Natalia Bondarchuk).

The British DVD release of *Mirror* contains two sound mixes, and they are very different. For instance, the 5.1 mix has far stronger music, and different mixes of the music and sound effects.

2

THE POETRY OF CINEMA

In all these ways the ordinary commercial cinema maintains something at least of the fullness of the primal myth, blending, in various permutations, fact, drama, the 'Surreal', dream, magic and the supernatural powers of their play. Perhaps we too readily assume the mass media's lack of, and antagonism towards, poetry...

Raymond Durgnat (238)

The cinema should always be the discovery of something. I believe that the cinema should be essentially poetic.

Orson Welles

If you think of *Mirror* as a *poem*, it all makes sense. Everything. Cinema poeticizes reality and the real. The filmmaker may not intend poetry, but, as in Eisensteinian montage, the effect, as far as the viewer is concerned, can be poetic. The images, the colours, the textures, the manipulation of time, the multiple viewpoints, the metaphors and connections made – all these can be made poetic. Certainly the films of Charlie Chaplin, Milos Forman, Atom Egoyam, Ermanno Olmi, Douglas Sirk and Li Shao-hong, six very different filmmakers, contain moments of intense poetry. When the subject is bleak, such as poverty-stricken childhood (as in Bill Douglas's childhood trilogy), or cannibalism (as in *Weekend* [Jean-Luc Godard, 1967, France] or in *Blow Out* [*La Grande Boufe*, Marco Ferrerii, 1973, Italy]), the results can still be very poetic. If lyricism is in the perception of the beholder, then any (and every) film can be poetic. Often it is the movies that strive self-consciously to be lyrical that fail: the mythopœic experience can be elusive.

Like poetry, cinema is full of rhymes, of dissonances, assonances, cross-references, plots and subplots. Like poetry, cinema uses images, motifs, metaphors, allusions, allegories, repetitions, fables, refrains, subjective viewpoints, lyricism and so on. Many moviemakers, like most poets, have their own vocabulary, full of their own words (or shots), their own phrases (or camera movements, lighting styles) and their own quotes (or *hommages*, as the French New Wave filmmakers called them). A platitude of the critical academy is that writers have to establish their own 'voice', that the most successful artists have personal vision. Each of cinema's *auteurs* has her/ his own 'voice' – Andrei Tarkovsky has his long, water-filled takes; Shoji Kawamori with his intense ærial battles; Ingmar Bergman has his ensemble playing, Expressionist camera and alienated winterscapes; Sergei Eisenstein has his montage, and so on.

In a 1964 essay, Andrei Tarkovsky said he wanted cinema to fuse the subjective and the objective, to be both facts and feelings, to have its own poetic logic, to have its own form, separate from literature or theatre, and to express the 'poetic concreteness' of dreams. Poetry, Tarkovsky asserted in *Sculpting In Time* (21), is 'an awareness of the world, a particular way of relating to reality. So poetry becomes a philosophy to guide a man throughout his life'. For Tarkovsky, poetic thinking (intuitive, subjective, associative) may be closer to life, and to thought itself, than the narrative logic of traditional drama (and cinema), which was the only model used for expressing dramatic conflict. It was cinema's task, Tarkovsky reckoned, to convey some of the impressions, the associations, the memories and subjective states of life (ST, 23).

Andrei Tarkovsky made suddenly thrilling evocations one of his specialities: a shot of trees rustling in the wind at night, from Tarkovsky's *Mirror*, or the snow falling at the end of *Nostalghia*. The Tarkovsky shock moment was a set-piece that often revelled in the self-conscious fakery of cinema. But it is the images that do the talking, that stay in the mind, that creep in under the mundane architecture of dialogue, characters, action and plot.

ANDREI TARKOVSKY AS POET

For Andrei Tarkovsky, poetic cinema is subjective, intuitive, non-rational, non-literary. It begins and ends with an individual's perception (ST, 20). For Tarkovsky, ever the Renaissance philosopher, the individual is the measure of everything. Thus, Tarkovsky rejects logic, classical drama, cause-and-effect and simplistic notions of narration. Tarkovsky exalts dream-logic (what Elisabeth Sewell in *The Orphic Voice* called 'post-logic'), poetic associations, non-linearity, and the primacy of the individual response. 'Poetic cinema' is the best term for his kind of cinema. He defines it thus:

> I find poetic links, the logic of poetry in cinema, extraordinarily pleasing. They seem to me perfectly appropriate to the potential of cinema as the most truthful and poetic of art forms. (ST, 18)

Andrei Tarkovsky's concept of poetic cinema is the same as his concept of art: he exalts the spiritual, the search for 'truth', subjectivity and so on. Tarkovsky forces cinema to become increasingly dream-like. Tarkovsky blurs the boundaries of dream and actuality. As Robert Bresson put it: '[y]our film must resemble what you see on shutting your eyes' (50). For Ingmar Bergman, Tarkovsky was the master of dream films: 'Tarkovsky is the greatest of them all. He moves with such naturalness in the room of dreams…'[1]

Pier Paolo Pasolini developed one of the most sophisticated theories of the poetry of cinema. For Pasolini, cinema was 'substantially and naturally

---
1 In N. Sinyard, 1992, 47.

poetic', because it was dream-like,[2] and because things in themselves were 'profoundly poetic'. In Pasolini's poetics of cinema, reality and cinema commingle, as a system of signs.

> The cinema is a language which expresses reality with reality. So the question is: what is the difference between the cinema and reality? Practically none.

To express people, Pier Paolo Pasolini used people; to express trees, Pasolini used real trees, as he found them in reality. 'Cinema represents reality with reality; it is metonymic and not metaphoric'. Yes but exactly what 'reality' is, and what 'reality' is in cinema, is difficult to define, Pasolini admitted. The first question to ask when people use terms like 'reality' or 'realism' is: *whose reality? Whose realism?*

For Barthelemy Amengual, Andrei Tarkovsky's cinema is like Byzantine icons: 'the icon transposes the spiritual into physical space; Tarkovsky transposes it into physical time'.[3] In his magisterial book on Yasujiro Ozu, David Bordwell suggested that Ozu's art

> like that of Bresson and Dreyer [one could also include Tarkovsky], evokes the ineffable as a by-product of remarkably constrained and exact choices. The point is not what it means but what it *does*: train us in nuance, suggest new possibilities for ordering experience, and – not least – invite us to contemplate the possibilities of the film medium when it is no longer subordinated to story construction. (140)

That approach helps with looking at Andrei Tarkovsky's cinema: if one considers what it *does* not what it *means*: instead of trying to decipher the rain, smoke, horses and other Tarkovsky motifs and symbols, turning them into categories of written or verbal language, accept them as experiences or effects. That is, of course, the overriding project of one strain of contemporary cultural theory which reckons that questions like 'what does it mean?' are no longer

---
[2] 'Cinema is already a dream'.
[3] B. Amengual: "Andrei Tarkovski après sept films", in M. Estève, 1983.

significant. More to the point is: 'what does it feel like?', and: 'what is its effect?' And Tarkovsky's films work elegantly on both these levels, on the levels of meaning and doing (and on other levels, too).

Andrei Tarkovsky speaks of cinema in terms of poetry and music. Like music, he says, cinema needs no mediating language: it deals with reality (ST, 176-7). 'I classify cinema and music among the *immediate* artforms since they need no mediating language' (ST, 176). That's Pasolini's notion, again: cinema and reality commingle.

Any passage taken at random from *Sculpting in Time* gives a clear sense of Andrei Tarkovsky's notions of art: '[a]rt is born and takes hold wherever there is a timeless and insatiable longing for the spiritual' (ST, 38). Tarkovsky saw himself within Alexandre Astruc's *camera-stylo/ auteur* theory tradition. Tarkovsky is a *ciné*-poet *par excellence*, a filmmaker who takes Dziga Vertov's *kino-glaz* ('cinema-eye') and theory of *kino-pravda* ('cinema-truth') to the point of mysticism. Tarkovsky's cinema is more mystical than most, in the true meaning of the word. Not 'mystical' because it is strange, unreal, poetic or even religious, in the traditional sense, but 'mystical' because his cinema constantly strives, like authentic mysticism, for something wholly other, for the numinous, the divine, the beyond.

THE POETRY OF *MIRROR*

In *Sculpting in Time,* Andrei Tarkovsky describes how *Mirror* was transformed from being a series of somewhat unconnected memories and feelings of childhood to complexly interwoven webs of scenes, shots, episodes, gestures, newsreels, past and present experiences (*Mirror* was co-written with Alexander Misharin). He wrote:

> This account of the making of *Mirror* illustrates that for me scenario is a fragile, living, ever-changing structure, and that a film is only made at the moment when work on it is finally completed. (ST, 131)

Mirror only started to become a good film during the editing (according to Andrei Tarkovsky), which Tarkovsky and the editing team (led by Lyudmilla Feiginova) spent a lot of time on (however, one imagines that the beauty of the rushes must have been obvious to anyone who saw them). For Tarkovsky, cinema is not literature, as poetry is not prose. Cinema transforms literature into another medium. A movie such as *Mirror* is intensely poetic, and lives in a different world from literature, from the printed word. There are incidents in it that are found in literature – the return of the father, for example, to his homeland and family. But this is filmed as one shot (the father in uniform holding his estranged children) in a complex montage which cuts between past and present and two images by Leonardo da Vinci accompanied by the strains of an opera singing of the veil of the temple being rent. Time and space are squashed through the eye of the needle of Tarkovsky's cinematic virtuosity, and changed utterly. The script might be born in prose and literature, but after cinematic transformation it ends up as something else entirely – a series of images and sounds. The poetry of cinema takes over.

ANDREI TARKOVSKY AND THE HISTORY OF POETRY

In his movies Andrei Tarkovsky quoted poets such as Aleksandr Pushkin, Fyodor Tyutchev, William Shakespeare and, above all, his father, Arseny Tarkovsky (not to be confused with Aleksandr Tvardovsky, 1910-71). Ironically, the general public in Russia knew about Tarkovsky and his films before Tarkovsky senior and his poetry (so that Arseny Tarkovsky was known as the father of Tarkovsky the film director, not the other way around).[4]

Arseny Tarkovsky (who died in 1989), was a poet who remained unpublished during Andrei Tarkovsky's childhood. Today, Tarkovsky senior is regarded as a significant poet, though definitely not to be classed among the greats of modern Russia like, say, Aleksandr Pushkin, Alexander Blok or Yevgeny Yvetushenko. Tarkovsky's poetry is essentially lyrical – poetry in the classical sense: impressionistic experiences of the world (it's poetry in the wake of Rainer Maria Rilke, Stéphane Mallarmé and Paul Valéry). It does not have a self-conscious ideological or political agenda, for instance. But it was hugely important for his son's films: when Andrei Tarkovsky quotes from a poet, it is from Arseny Tarkovsky more than any other (though he does quote from Pushkin and Fyodor Tyuchev. Pushkin is one of Tarkovsky's poetry gods: Pushkin's poem 'The Prophet' was one of Tarkovsky's key poetic inspirations). A school friend (Yuri Kochevrin) recalled that Tarkovsky carried a book of Tarkovsky senior's poetry with him all the time (JP, 19).

Andrei Tarkovsky's father's poetry influenced much of Tarkovsky's cinema. It's easy to spot the influence of the conservative, classical, musical and metaphysical style of Tarkovsky senior in his son's movies. Tarkovsky not only incorporated his father's poetry into the background and tone of his films, he also included them in the soundtrack and dialogue, most prominently in *Mirror* and *Nostalghia*. The first poem in *Zerkalo* (read by his father) is probably the best, most moving Arseny Tarkovsky poem appearing in a Tarkovsky movie: 'First Meeting' (published in 1962):

> Every moment that we were together
> Was a celebration, like Epiphany,
> In all the world the two of us alone,
> You were bolder, lighter than a bird-wing,
> Heady as vertigo you ran downstairs
> Two steps at a time, and led me
> Through damp lilac, into your domain

---

[4] M. Turovskaya, 15.

On the other side, beyond the mirror. (ST, 101)

The 1975 movie goes on to trace the life led 'beyond the mirror'. After his father Arseny, Aleksandr Pushkin is Andrei Tarkovsky's main poetic influence (or most often cited). In poems such as 'Autumn', Pushkin created the dream of a mythical, snowbound Russia:

> O mournful season! How enchanting to the eye! Your beauty with its message of farewell delights me: I love nature's sumptuous fading, the woods clothed in purple and gold, the noise of the wind and the fresh breeze in the tree-tops, the skies covered with rolling mist, the infrequent sun-ray, the first frost, and the distant threat of hoary winter.[5]

This is the mist-soaked Russia that Andrei Tarkovsky portrays in *Andrei Roublyov*, *Mirror* and *Nostalghia*. In *Mirror* the boy quotes Aleksandr Pushkin's letter of October 19, 1836 to Piotr Chadayev on the founding of Russia (ST, 195). Tarkovsky's poetic cinema is part of the Russian poetic tradition, and Pushkin is the spirit and apotheosis of Russian poetry. Tarkovsky worked in that Russian lyrical tradition, which runs from Pushkin and Fyodor Tyutchev through Alexander Blok, Anna Akhmatova, Boris Pasternak, Osip Mandelstam and Sergei Esenin, to Arseny Tarkovsky and Yevgeny Yvetushenko.

One can see similarities between Andrei Tarkovsky's art and the cosmological visions of Dante in his *Divina Commedia*; with William Shakespeare's tragic humanism; with the religious fervour of the British Metaphysical poets (John Donne, George Herbert, Richard Crashaw and Henry Vaughan); with the nature-loving pantheism of Romantics such as Novalis, Friedrich Hölderlin, Johann Wolfgang von Goethe and William Wordsworth; with the musicality and linguistic philosophies of the French Symbolists (Paul Verlaine, Stephane Mallarmé, Paul Valéry and Stefan George); and with modern, European poets such as St-John Perse, Paul Celan and Georg Trakl.

One of the key works of literature that Andrei

---

5 A. Pushkin, in D. Obolensky, 108.

Tarkovsky quotes from in his films is the *Bible*. After the *Bible*, William Shakespeare, Aleksandr Pushkin and Fyodor Mikhaylovich Dostoievsky are favourites. *Don Quixote* is referenced in *Solaris*; Fyodor Tyuchev in *Stalker*; Anton Chekhov, Dante Alighieri (the *Inferno*), Dostoievsky (*The Devils*), Arseny Tarkovsky and Pushkin in *Mirror*. In his book on cinema, *Sculpting In Time*, Tarkovsky frequently refers to literary figures: apart from the ones cited above are Boris Pasternak, Osip Mandelstham, Nikolai Gogol, Ivan Bunin, Alexander Herzen, Alexander Blok, Vyacheslav Ivanov and Nikolai Gumilyov among Russian writers and poets, and Hermann Hesse, G.W.F. Hegel, Paul Valéry, Ernest Hemingway, Emile Zola, Gustave Flaubert, Johann Wolfgang von Goethe, Dante Alighieri, Thomas Mann, Franz Kafka, and Marcel Proust among international writers.

Tarkovsky at work: shooting *Mirror* (his mother's on the left).

Tarkovsky on the set of Mirror

3

TARKOVSKY'S SYMBOLS

Cinema is life.

Jean-Luc Godard

No other filmmaker uses rain, water, fire or flight in the same, idiosyncratic, hypnotic and profound way as Andrei Tarkovsky. The way these motifs or symbols are used is distinctly Tarkovskyan, setting him apart from other filmmakers. Yet Tarkovsky denies that these elements are 'symbols' – he dislikes symbols, metaphors, parables and fantasies. He acknowledges the power of dreams, the occurrence of miracles, the movement of inanimate objects and the existence of God, but he denies symbols and metaphors. Yet he so deliberately and self-consciously places fire or water in his filmic spaces. Often these 'motifs' appear on cue, timed to make the biggest impact – such as the rain falling at the end of *Stalker*, after the men have stopped fighting. The rain here, at this point in the film, is the re-affirmation of nature and the natural forces of life. It washes away the delusions, the anxieties, the narcissisms of the three seekers, re-aligning their expectations. The rainfall through the smashed roof of the building next to the Room in the Zone makes the water glitter, and it sounds refreshing and calming. The rain brings them back to the fundamentals of life. It reminds them of simple but important things. Rain happens no matter what humans do or think or feel.

Certainly Andrei Tarkovsky's motifs act on the symbolic level, as well as the concrete level and the dramatic level. The motifs play a part in the dramatic narrative of the film, but they also work on the symbolic, spiritual, social and ideological levels. Asked if there was any symbolism in *Mirror*, Tarkovsky replied:

> No! The images themselves are like symbols, but unlike accepted symbols they cannot be deciphered. The image is like a clot of life, and even the author may not be able to work out what it means, let alone the audience. (D, 369)

But symbols are not meant to be 'deciphered'. Part of their power is that they go beyond rationalization. Andrei Tarkovsky is digging himself into a hermeneutic hole by claiming there is no symbolism in his movies. There is, masses of it.

With Andrei Tarkovsky's poetic cinema, one is sure the motifs are there for a purpose, and have a special value, symbolic or concrete or spiritual or otherwise, as may be, for the director. Of *Mirror* Tarkovsky wrote that 'there is no hidden, coded meaning in the film, nothing beyond the desire to tell the truth' (ST, 133). Yet this is the movie with more Tarkovskyan motifs than any other: rain, water, fire, paintings, birds, wind and flying.

RAIN.

The one emblem that Andrei Tarkovsky probably uses more than any other is rain. Traditionally, rain symbolizes beautitude, purification, fecundity, revelation, divinity, and blessing (J. Cooper, 136). Clearly, rain doesn't 'mean' or evoke all these things in Tarkovsky's metaphysical cinema. Yet it is no coincidence that rain presides over much of the childhood *dacha* scenes in *Mirror* (and *Nostalghia*). In *Mirror*, the ruler of the Narrator's childhood is his mother. She is deified, filmed in a number of glorifying poses and lighting designs which exalt her as a Goddess. In *Mirror*'s opening image, she sits on the fence, presiding over that huge field of buckwheat, and the trees of the Ignatievo forest behind her (lyrically evoked in Andrei's father's poetry). She is an agricultural Goddess, an Earth Mother. So it's only natural that it rains here, for as Aeschlyus says: '[t]he rain, falling from the sky, impregnates the earth, so that she gives birth to plants and grain for man and beast' (in ib., 136).

The first mysterious event in *Mirror*, the house on fire, is framed by the rain dripping from the roof. Later, the mother washes her hair and the room rains; she runs to work through the rain; and at the printing works the water runs out on her in the shower. In this and other films, rain is a purifying and regenerating element, often associated with childhood, parents and sexuality. In *Solaris*, at the end, rain pours into the father's house, and the self-absorbed patriarch doesn't notice it. In *Stalker*, masculinist/ patriarchal science (the nuclear bomb) is broken up ritually, and thrown into the feminine pool of regeneration; then comes that lengthy rainfall; each protagonist muses on their life and future. In *Andrei Roublyov* and *Ivan's Childhood,* rain seems not to have so much of a symbolic purpose, even though it begins and ends on cue, as it does at the beginning of *Solaris*, when the father steps inside the house to avoid a shower. However, it is raining during Ivan's third dream, on the apple truck (rain heightened the dream's significance). And in *Andrei Roublyov,* rain appears at many key moments: the rain shower with the three monks at the beginning; the flashback Roublyov has; when Boriska finds the right kind of clay; and running down the paintings and the horses in the rain in the epilogue. Once again, the cinema of Sergei Paradjanov is linked to the rain in Tarkovsky's films: both directors are very fond of it.

WATER.

The half-soaked landscapes (or half-dry water-scapes) reflect the in-between-worlds nature of the Tarkovskyan protagonist's predicament. The pools obscure reality and also invigorate it. Water runs down roads and – much stranger – down walls. *Mirror* features a whole room of wet walls. The mother (as wife here) has just washed her hair – she stands back and flails her arms mysteriously. Suddenly the room is full of rain and the ceiling starts caving in. Clearly this dream-rain refers to some powers or influences Maria has – powers over her husband, and over her son, who is the implied voyeur (like the viewer) of this bizarre scene (the scene portrays the estranged (yet erotic) relationship between the mother and the father). The woman, shaman-like, conjures up this psychic rainfall (or her state expands poetically to include the whole room, and by extension, the whole world). In the corner of the room a flame flickers. Fire and water are similarly pointed up in the scene a few minutes earlier, when the neighbour's house burns.

FIRE.

Andrei Tarkovsky uses fire in an alchemical fashion: he burns it on screen in the hope of alchemically forging another element – preferably the Philosopher's Stone or a magical child, if not some cinematic gold. In *Mirror*, fire – in a field or in a grate – is the image that connects past and present, that binds space and time. The image of a hand warming itself functions like the dog in *Nostalghia*, it jogs the memory and induces the flight from the present into the past.

There is an explicit religious dimension to the burning bush in *Mirror* – the Narrator and his wife discuss the Biblical source of the burning bush. During this conversation the camera lingers on the Narrator's wife: this is significant, because the episode of God talking to Moses through a burning bush (*Exodus*, 3:2) relates to the sacred virginity of the Virgin Mary. The mother in *Mirror* is again likened to the Mother of Jesus (as are the mother and Eugenia in *Nostalghia*). Like the burning bush, the Madonna remained intact[1] (J. Metford, 56). It is another example of the Goddess symbolism in the film. The relevant extract from the *Bible* runs thus:

> And the angel of the Lord appeared unto him [Moses] in a flame of fire out of the midst of a bush; and he looked, and, behold, the bush burned with fire, and the bush was not

[1] It's a symbolic innocence when applied to the mother in *Mirror*.

consumed. (*Exodus*, 2:3)

There is religious continuity here, over five thousand years: Moses sees God in the burning bush, and the camera tracks to the window of an apartment in modern Moscow, and outside is a burning bush.

WIND AND AIR.

With most movie-makers, blowing wind could not be counted as a 'symbol' or 'motif'. Yet a wind machine is usually necessary for an Andrei Tarkovsky production (Hong Kong filmmakers such as Tony Ching, Tsui Hark and Yuen Woo-ping use wind machines in every single scene, including static interior scenes). In *The Sacrifice*, for instance, there is an (imagined?) atomic blast wave that blows away some snow and old doors. There are two gusts of a breeze at the beginning of *Mirror*, which at first are simply mysterious, simply *there*. But the prologue of *Mirror* features a stutterer being 'cured'; and, after the wind has gone, the mother turns away and the poetry begins. Here the narrative proper of *Mirror* begins: and it is the Creative Word through air which has set it in motion: from the stuttering youth, through the title sequence, to the breeze in the field to the spoken words of the poetry, the gusts of the creative spirit blow through the film.

Wind and air is the spirit, the *pneuma*, the breath of life, associated with procreation (in Aristotle), orgasm and the soul. Wind or breath is part of the same holy male mystery of fire. One recalls that in *Mirror* fire suggests the father or the Narrator (the son of the present) remembering, and that rain and water relates to the mother (or feminine principle). This fits; the pieces of *Mirror*'s jigsaw start to lock together, in a poetic manner because wind and air fans and feeds fire (air/wind and fire are always in a relationship). Indeed, the five-year-old boy thinks immediately of his father when he hears the rustling bushes outside his bedroom. Editor Lyudmilla Feiginova comes back to this shot a few times: by day or night (sometimes in slow motion, sometimes in black-and-white); one sees the trees and bushes next to the house blowing in the breeze. This is an image of otherness – the primal, implacable, untameable otherness of the natural world. But it also evokes the father, and what he brings with him – the otherness of the outside world, in a realm of exile, of marginality. He exists in the outer spaces, like Cathy's ghost in *Wuthering Heights*.

HOUSE.

The primary Tarkovskyan environment is the house of childhood, the Russian *dacha* in the countryside, which appears in most of Andrei Tarkovsky's films, but most fully realized in *Mirror*. This house is explored endlessly by the roving camera, which tracks around the rooms and picks out *that* particular table from memory and *this* magical window with its view over the buckwheat field and *those* bushes outside and the forest beyond.

ANGEL.

The ancestors of the angel in Western religion is again the archaic shamen, who danced like birds and donned costumes of feathers (the Native American feathered headdress is a late example of the bird-shaman's regalia). Birds and women are again connected in *Mirror*: the mother kills the cockerel; a bird breaks the pane of glass in the *dacha*; a bird flaps beside the floating woman. Most oddly of all, a bird lands on Asafyev's head, a miraculous shot. A bird represents the soul very clearly in the Narrator's grandiose act of the setting free of the tiny bird (a sparrow) that he's been holding on his death bed.

The scene of Gorchakov's soliloquy in 1983's *Nostalghia* is announced by the incredible imagery of a statue of an angel under water. The shot begins with a slow tilt up to reveal Gorchakov wading through a stream, on his way to the flooded church. The stream, fringed with long grass, recalls the opening shots of *Solaris*. Gorchakov, in voiceover, recites Arseny

Tarkovsky's poem "As a child I once fell ill" (ST, 91), a scene that was originally meant to go in *Mirror*. A young girl, called Angela (another reference to angels), is seen climbing around the walls of the flooded church (in the script, it's a 12 year-old boy, called Marco [CS, 494]). Gorchakov's long sermon, partly in Italian, partly in Russian, is delivered from the centre of the pool in the drowned church. He stands knee-deep in water. The place is full of dripping water. It starts to rain.

THE LOOKING GLASS: MIRRORS IN *MIRROR*

No object seems more suited to cinema than the mirror (as image, theme, motif, philosophy, etc). Andrei Tarkovsky is by no means the only filmmaker to be fascinated by mirrors: consider the *Orpheus* movies directed by Jean Cocteau, where characters step backwards into mirrors on their way to the Underworld, or the moment in *2,001: A Space Odyssey*, where astronaut Bowman contemplates himself in horror after travelling through the Stargate. The mirror is the perfect object for embodying modernism, whether it is used in Egon Schiele's stylized self-portraits, André Gide's self-reflexive *mise-en-âbyme* fiction, or the films of Ingmar Bergman, Rainer Maria Fassbinder, Orson Welles, and the Marx Brothers.

In *Mirror* the mirror functions as a poetic interface between past and present – this is made clear when, after the raining room sequence, the mother looks at herself in the mirror, then she's seen as an old woman: she wipes the mirror. The movie subsequently travels, as the first poem says, 'beyond the mirror'.

> *Take the mirror as your master – I mean smooth-surfaced mirrors – for when reflected on their surface objects resemble paintings in many ways. Thus, painting shows the object on a level surface, yet they look as if they were in relief, and the mirror does the same. Painting is based on the surface only and so is the mirror.*

Leonardo da Vinci[2]

Cameras can look into mirrors and one can't tell which is the reflection and which is the 'reality'. Cameras love mirrors, and make love with mirrors. Virtual, cyborg, real, dream, imaginary or contrived reality – all these blur in cinema. Only when the camera pulls back from a mirror can one see which side is which. Hundreds of filmmakers have exploited this kind of manipulation. The mirror is the perfect device for Jean-Luc Godard's postmodern explorations, where scenes are acted into mirrors (as in *Vivre Sa Vie*, 1962, France). At the beginning of *Peggy Sue Got Married* (Francis Coppola, 1986, U.S.A.), the godfather-director has a double mimic the motions of the lead actress (Kathleen Turner) making herself up in a dressing table mirror, echoing the finest mirror gag in movie history – when Harpo skillfully imitates Groucho's every movement in *Duck Soup* (Leo McCarey, 1933, U.S.A.).

In *Nostalghia*, Gorchakov stares into a mirror on a wardrobe in the street and finds his *doppelgänger*, Domenico, staring back at him (it was a scene that came from the days of *Mirror*). This is a common motif of identification. At the end of the 1983 film, as the camera slowly zooms out from the house and Gorchakov, the first indication the audience has that he is not back in Russia is from the reflection of the arches of the Cathedral in the pool in front of him. This sense of unease is exacerbated even further: the camera is set up so that where the reflection of the Russian house should be, in the pool, one sees the Cathedral: this reflection accentuates the unreality of Gorchakov's state of mind, and the ambiguity of his nostalgic achievement. Cinema is automatically nostalgic, Tarkovsky reckoned, due to its ability to replay the same scenes again and again (ST, 140).

In *Solaris*, the mirrors are of a different order: there are the circular windows that look out onto the vortex of

---

[2] In V. Stoichita, 12.

the Ocean; and the video screens which reflect back a different kind of image. In *The Sacrifice*, Alex is filmed in mirrors, and the *Adoration of the Magi* reproduction in Little Man's room is shot under glass so it acts as a mirror. Meanwhile, the floor of the main room downstairs is so highly polished it acts as a mirror. Often in Andrei Tarkovsky's films, characters stare at themselves in mirrors, in fascination, sometimes in vanity (adjusting their appearance), but also in fear, as if they're seeing something truly other. In the unmade *Hoffmanniana*, the mirror is the familiar seeing device of fairy tales: Hoffmann sees himself creeping down a corridor carrying a candle (CS, 348).

Stuart Hancock noted that:

Mirrors abound in [Tarkovsky's] films, and often his characters speak to one another's mirror image rather than to each other. In carefully staged scenes, characters stare off in different directions, aiming their words into thin air, even though those words work into each other's hearts like daggers. (1996)

In film after film, Andrei Tarkovsky's camera dwells on reflections in water, and often water and glass together. There are glass jars and bottles scattered on the floor of Domenico's house in *Nostalghia*; and a large jar or bottle features in the childhood sequences of *Mirror*. In *The Sacrifice* glasses tremble and a jar of milk smashes. In *Solaris* the chandelier rattles. At the end of *Stalker* the glasses which at the beginning trembled as the train trundled by, skid along a table (perhaps thru telekinesis). Fish swim in a glass bowl, itself afloat, in the Stalker's dream.

Glass objects – in the form of bottles, cups, mirrors, vases, or jugs – are part of Andrei Tarkovsky's large props bag of still-life artefacts, which he sets up on table tops, or chairs, or window sills: eggs, books, plants, candles, lamps, drapes, lace and bed sheets.

Glass is often associated with death (in European fairy tales and Celtic mythology), the double or twin, as well as Buddhist transparency, self-awareness, celestial power, purity, perfection, the light of God and the self-luminous. Water and glass possess magic for Andrei Tarkovsky. He makes glass appear like some strange element, some new addition to the Periodic Table of elements of science. The glass containers in his movies look like the precious phials, crucibles and vessels of some mediæval alchemist or magus – snatched from the laboratories of alchemists Paracelsus or Cornelius Agrippa, say. The mirrors and glasses are filters, veils, barriers, walls enclosing secret worlds beyond reach. One can't quite cross the threshold of the mirror in Tarkovsky's cinema, as one can in Jean Cocteau's *Orpheus* films.

DREAMS.

The journey in *Mirror* is the complex flight between past and present, between memory, dream and fantasy, between wife and mother, between youth and age, between the family then and the family now.

Generally, Andrei Tarkovsky sticks to straightforward dream or memory sequences: it is assumed that Gorchakov's dreams in *Nostalghia*, for instance, are what he is really dreaming about (the dreams are not simply Gorchakov's memories, though: the viewer isn't asked to assume that the *dacha*, the trees, the pool, the dog and the groups of women in Gorchakov's dreams are what his life in Russia is *really* like). Tarkovsky always investigates the past, how memories of happier times haunt the protagonist (like Ivan's dreams of his mother in *Ivan's Childhood*). His films do not use flashforwards, for instance, of what the future might be like for the characters (in *Nostalghia*, though, Gorchakov has a vision of Eugenia and his wife, the embodiments (the spirits, the *anima*) of Italy and Russia, embracing). And Tarkovsky's films do not (usually) insert flash cuts to confuse the audience: his memory and dream sequences are usually clearly signposted as such (in *The Sacrifice* and *Nostalghia*, though, the segues between 'reality' and dreams are more ambiguous). In *Mirror*, it is more complex, because some of the dreams or memory sequences are not wholly from the Narrator's (Alexei's) point-of-view. The flashback to Maria's ominous experience in the printing works, for instance, is not something the Narrator had direct access to (as with the newsreels).

Each Andrei Tarkovsky movie has a mythic structure. *Mirror* relates to *Hamlet* and *Oedipus Rex*, with œdipal and maternal material particularly prominent. Like *Solaris*, *Mirror*'s about being haunted by the past, about being unable escape the past, or transcend one's origins. *Stalker* has elements of the *Odyssey* and Greek myths in it, as well as many Biblical overtones (for instance, Ancient Greek mythological quests such as Jason and the Golden Fleece, or Orpheus in the Underworld, or Odysseus travelling back to Ithaca).

SEX.

The sexual act in Andrei Tarkovsky's cinema is portrayed by flying or floating. When Alex makes love with the witch Maria in *Offret*, she strips her clothes off and caresses him like a mother tending a child. They rise off the bed, spinning slowly. The lights dim gradually and the room becomes a womb. It's more like a regression to early childhood than sex between adults, more like a mother comforting a son (look at – or listen to – the way Alex behaves in this scene). The sex act is elevated from the realm of realism to the mythic, transcendent realm. (The links between flying and erection, intercourse and orgasm were pointed out by Sigmund Freud, among others. What's great about Tarkovsky's cinema is that he can take something as obvious as flying = sex and make it work. It could so easily backfire, and come across as a crude joke).[3]

The floating scene in *Mirror* is more explicit. The father turns to the woman floating above the bed and strokes her hand. It is one of the few obvious gestures of affection in Andrei Tarkovsky's *œuvre*. The woman says 'it's as though I'm floating in the air.' She looks dreamy, or post-orgasmic, lying on her side, her body twisted,

---
[3] In the *Aquarion Evol anime* series, when the hero is aroused he flies.

her hair floating behind her.

The scene is made clearly erotic by the moment that precedes it: Maria has just killed a cockerel. She stares into the camera and smiles wickedly, evilly, triumphantly. Her face is lit starkly from below, accentuating the sockets of her eyes, recalling the manic stares of the alter-egos in the films directed by Stanley Kubrick: Jack Torrance, Dave Bowman and Alex the droog. On a number of occasions, in *2001: A Space Odyssey* (1968, U.S.A.), *A Clockwork Orange* (1972, U.S.A.) and *The Shining* (1980, U.S.A.), Kubrick has his anti-heroes stare at the viewer in close-up, their heads lowered and lit from below, their eyes wide-open and staring intently.

This is how Maria looks at the viewer in *Mirror* after her act of violence. The wall behind her drips with water, recalling the hair-washing scene earlier, depicting the child's confused view of the sexual relations between his mother and father. Maria is transfigured – into a wraith. If ever the look of a castrating phallic mother or Medusa was portrayed in cinema, this is it. The sense of this complex montage is ambiguous. Certainly it's about violence, sex, blood, illness and heightened states of perception. The taunting look of Maria just after she's killed the cockerel suggests she's just dispatched her husband, or his sexuality, or his potency, or his identity, or her memory of it all. She kills the cockerel and it is an act of supremacy. The symbolism of the cockerel is, traditionally, solar, fertile, masculine and phallic. A Freudian analyst might treat the scene as a violent castration, recalling the Indian Goddesses who beheaded their consorts as they copulated with them.[4] Wendy O'Flaherty wrote in *Women, Androgynes, and Other Mythical Beasts*:

> The Goddess not only dominates her consort but kills him, cutting off his head. In this she resembles the female praying mantis, who bites off her consort's head... By eating his head, the mantis removes her consort's inhibitions and frees him to copulate more vigorously. (81)

---
[4] Wendy O'Flaherty, *Women, Androgynes, and Other Mythical Beasts*, University of Chicago Press, Chicago, IL, 1980, 46-47, 81-87.

Decapitation and castration are symbolically and mythopœically equivalent. The poetic implications of this scene are thus clear. Here the woman is mythicized as a monstrous Other, the castrating Goddess, the *vagina denta* or 'phallic mother' of psychoanalysis.

Andrei Tarkovsky was unhappy with the scene: he wanted to cut it because it was too obvious what was going on (ST, 109-110). But it's been known all through the film that the woman Maria (like Natalia, her modern-day counterpart) has been much more powerful, more independent, more noble, and more resourceful than her husband. When the father returns from the war he stands meekly with his children (he's given nothing to 'do' by the director); Maria, meanwhile is a restless, dynamic character. The first time Maria's seen in *Mirror* she is sitting on the fence; then she walks to the house; then she stands in the corner of the room; she walks about; sits and stares out of the window; goes out to the fire. She is not 'motherly' in the usual, stereotypical, traditional sense of the term. She is not shown doing domestic chores, or talking to or cuddling her children (or even being much aware of them). It is the aunt, not the mother, who picks up and looks after the children. The mother is restless, dissatisfied, sometimes portrayed as beautiful, other times as unkempt and ugly. Part of her remains other, a mystery to her children.

Images from Andrei Tarkovsky's other movies: Ivan's Childhood

Andrei Roublyov

Solaris

Stalker

Nostalghia

The Sacrifice – Tarkovsky does Bergman, again.

PART TWO

MIRROR

4

MIRROR

ZERKALO

We celebrated every moment
Of our meetings as epiphanies,
Just we two in all the world.
Bolder, lighter than a bird's wing,
You hurtled like vertigo
Down the stairs, leading
Through moist lilac to your realm
Beyond the mirror.

Arseny Tarkovsky, 'First Meetings'[1]

MIRROR AND POETRY

Mirror (*Zerkalo* or *The Bright, Bright Day*) is a poem. This is the key to understanding the film. It is a *ciné-poem*, complete with metaphors, allusions, references, historicity, lyricism, concrete and abstract images, a number of voices, motifs and symbols, autobiography, stanzas and refrains. Some images correspond to a line in a poem, while the refrains and links are the shots of fire which fade to black, or the b/w images of the trees in slow motion. If one thinks of *Mirror* poetically, then the form – the overlapping, the montages, the merging of imagery and events from the past and present – becomes clear. The spectator has to make an effort to unravel the components of the piece, has to fill in gaps and re-order the events, but it makes sense in the end.

Mirror begins with one of the most poetic ten or

[1] A. Tarkovsky, *Life, Life*, 42.

fifteen minutes in cinema: from the moment where Maria is sitting on the fence, to the house on fire, then after that to the hair-washing and rain-filled room sequence. There is so much going on, so much that is startling. Only a few movies – like *The Magnificent Ambersons* or *Akira* – have a similarly miraculous first reel. Oliver Assays reckoned (in 1997) that the post-credits sequence is 'one of the most beautiful things I had ever seen in the movies' (1997, 24). Absolutely.

Mirror is Andrei Tarkovsky's beloved project, one he (seems to have) wanted to make for a long time (it remained his favourite movie, and closest to his concept of cinema [CS, 255]). It is loosely autobiographical, and combines many elements, from poetry read in voiceover by the director's father Arseny Tarkovsky, to dream sequences, flashbacks, newsreels and mnemonics (memory devices). The film is a poetic exploration of childhood: the long dolly shots around the old house in the country and the Moscow apartment explore the spaces of childhood, the geography of memory: the table was there, the chair was here, the window was there, and so on. A film of acutely remembered places. Film as personal psycho-geography, self-reflexive, even indulgent, recalling *Otto e Mezzo* (1963) and *Amarcord* (1973), classics of the autobiographical or personal film genre directed by Federico Fellini.[2] For Oliver Assayas, *Mirror* was about movie perception, a film which went *beyond* cinema, into 'issues of memory and remembrance, and the relationship between memory and perception' (1997, 24).

One of the fan letters (which Andrei Tarkovsky quoted in his diary) enthused about *Mirror*:

> it is your best film, it is a film about life, the most truthful and realistic film of life that we have ever seen. How is it that you have such amazingly subtle understanding of all the confusion, complexity and splendour of life? (D, 213)

'I believe if one tells the truth, some kind of inner truth, one will always be understood', Andrei Tarkovsky

---

[2] *Ulysses' Gaze* (Theo Angelopoulos, 1995) is another.

commented, *pace Mirror*. In cinema, Tarkovsky said he wanted both the documentary, factual approach, in which every detail must be accurate, and the emotional, subjective, inner truth.

(But although *Mirror* would be 'a film built in its entirety on personal experience' [D, 13], it wouldn't, as Andrei Tarkovsky maintained in *Sculpting In Time*, be Tarkovsky talking about himself. It was, rather, ultimately a movie about feelings: about his feelings towards his loved ones and relatives, and about his own inadequacy – 'my feeling of duty left unfulfilled' [ST, 134]).

In a 1975 interview, Andrei Tarkovsky said, *pace Mirror*, that

> there are no entertaining moments in the film. In fact I am categorically against entertainment in cinema: it is as degrading for the author as it is for the audience.

That's a typical Tarkovskyan comment (but he's totally wrong about entertainment, I think). Andre Tarkovsky also took a dim view of art's ability to educate, too: 'art cannot teach anyone anything, since in four thousand years humanity has learnt nothing at all' (ST, 50). Art shouldn't explain, or prove, or answer questions, Tarkovsky added (ST, 54).

PAST AND PRESENT, ACTORS AND DOUBLES

Some viewers and critics were confused by the use of the same actors for different roles in *Mirror* (even though this is a not uncommon strategy: it's used in the *Back To the Future* series [1985-90], for instance, and other time travel movies. A famous instance occurs in *The Wizard of Oz* [1939], although that's not time travel, but other worlds).

Part of the point of using the same actors and actresses for the mother/ wife and Narrator/ son is to show that the past and present are connected and interfuse. The present exists beside the past, not only in dreams and memories, but also in people, in their faces, personalities and actions. There is a historical, social and personal continuity. One cannot escape the influence of the past, and the same situations are re-enacted (for example, the 1930s family is broken, and the present-day husband and wife in the Seventies have parted). Cinema works at the point of viewing in a continuous present, yet it is always, as Jean Cocteau said, 'filmed death'. The past and present are bound up tightly together in the last shot of the film: Maria is there, and Maria as an old woman with Maria's two children (the old woman doubles as a grandmother). Matriarchy and female solidarity is affirmed, as is generation-to-generation continuity, ambiguity and sadness.

'I should like to ask you all not to be so demanding, and not to think of *Mirror* as a difficult film', Andrei Tarkovsky asserted in 1975. It is no more than a straightforward, simple story. It doesn't have to be made any more understandable.

Structurally, there are two moments in the past that are explored in *Mirror*: 1935-36, 1942-43, and the present day is 1974. The movie principally takes place in these *three* time zones (discounting the newsreels), and in, primarily, *two* locations: a modern day apartment in Moscow, where the Narrator lives (tho' he is not seen); and the *dacha* (= house) in the country, where the Narrator lived as a boy with his mother, while his father was away at war or in the armed services. Characters are compared to each other, while others are irreconcilably opposed. (The newsreels, though, are roughly chronological).

Past (1935 and 1942)		*Present (about 1974)*
Maria, the mother	>	Natalia, the modern wife/ mother

Children's grandmother >		Maria as an old woman (*and* the Narrator's mother)
Aleksei, aged 5 and Aleksei, aged 12	>	Ignat, aged 12
Father (soldier)	>	Aleksei, the Narrator

The mother and the boy of the past also dwell in the present. There are further complexities: Andrei Tarkovsky's real father Arseny reads his own poems (but the poetry in the film is not identified as by Arseny Tarkovsky), while Andrei Tarkovsky's own mother appears as the grandmother (Maria as an old woman), *and* the grandmother in the 1935-36 scenes (or she is Maria as an old woman transposed to the past). In addition, Ignat Daniltsev plays both Ignat and Aleksei. (And there are many scenes where either Natalia and Ignat are together, or Maria and Aleksei, both pairs are played by the same performers).

Pier Paolo Pasolini had cast his mother to play the aged Virgin Mary in *The Gospel According To Matthew* (1964) (and Martin Scorsese liked to use his mother in minor roles). Andrei Tarkovsky's own step-daughter (Olga Kizilova) was the red-haired beloved of the teenage Aleksei, and Tarkovsky's second wife, Larissa Tarkovskaya, played the doctor's wife, Nadezha.[3] The *dacha* of the past is built on (the foundations of) Tarkovsky's real childhood home (it was important for Tarkovsky to build his childhood house in the *exact* spot it had once stood). The film is one long evocation

---

[3] There's a disturbing element of the lecherous old man and voyeur in Tarkovsky's cinema, too. The eroticized red-haired girl with the chapped lip in *Mirror*, for instance, is a teenage object of sexual desire for both the middle-aged military instructor and the middle-aged Narrator (and she was played by Tarkovsky's own step-daughter). Then there's the young woman Martha in *The Sacrifice*, seen naked in Alexander's dreams (with hints of incestuous desires); and Alex makes love with a much younger woman.

of one person's childhood. It might have turned out self-indulgent and pretentious. Instead it is magnificent and profound.

The view of the greatest animator in the world, Hayao Miyazaki, is worth quoting here:

> I think it's impossible to do everything you want. You have to make such a movie in a different place from a movie which one or two million people pay to see and get satisfied. When I watch a movie such as Tarkovsky's *Stalker*, I feel 'this SOB is doing as he pleases!' I think he is such a talented guy.

The *Bright, Bright Day* version of the screenplay contained scenes which did not make it into the final cut (though the ending was much the same): the cemetery scene; the mother selling flowers in the war; the demolishing of a church cupola; the mother and sister at a hippodrome; and the father's description of battle casualties.

MIRROR AS SPIRITUAL (AUTO)BIOGRAPHY

The function of the image, as Gogol said, is to express life itself, not ideas or arguments about life. It does not signify life or symbolise it, but embodies it, expressing its uniqueness.

Andrei Tarkovsky, *Sculpting In Time* (111)

As an evocation of childhood, the yearning, mystery and pain of it, *Mirror* is unsurpassed in cinema. True, Andrei Tarkovsky and co-scripter Alexander Misharin do simplify things by missing out the agony of adolescence. Instead they choose two ages, five and twelve, in which children are still children, and not restless, disaffected, disappointed teenagers. The movie could be extended indefinitely through a variety of age ranges: 2, 8, 15, 19, 26, and so on. Tarkovsky also excludes a crucial part of childhood – education and school; also, the child's relations with other children. By leaving out school and friends, Tarkovsky presents a highly selective view of childhood. For Tarkovsky, childhood is largely a lonely experience, with parental affection a rarity.

Mirror also acts as the spiritual biography of an age: the eras of 1935-36 and 1942-43 are so poignantly evoked by the newsreels. These images, seemingly a world away from an intimate portrait of childhood, fuse beautifully with the rest of the film.[4] There are moments of forced symbolism – the Narrator releasing the bird, for instance, which is intended to relate to his death. It is a motif out of the dumbest pop promo.[5] The film, though, soars above pretension and artifice by the magnitude of its passion. There is no denying the lucidity and poetic authenticity of these mnemonic images. *Mirror* is the closest thing in cinema to a poem by Rainer Maria Rilke, Arthur Rimbaud or C.P. Cavafy, those masters of the poetry of nostalgia. Like the poesie of Rilke, Cavafy and Rimbaud, *Mirror* is a dense mesh of constellations of images and memories, a veritable mnemonic banquet. It is a film of fierce self-reflexive intensity – something like Rimbaud in his poem of childhood 'Le Poëtes de sept ans':

> At seven years old, he created novels of life
> In the great desert, where exiled Liberty gleams,
> Forests, suns, riverbanks, savannahs! – He was aided
> By illustrated magazines where, red-faced, he saw
> Spanish and Italian women laughing.[6]

Among the thousands of mainstream (Hollywood) films that try to depict children and childhood, very few come close to the luminous authenticity of *Mirror*. Yet *Mirror* never slips into easy sentimentality (although it does come close once or twice). It never becomes complacent or banal. It is marvellously self-reflexive, yet avoids all the traps of inward-looking art. Though unashamedly introspective, *Mirror* virtually achieves a

---

[4] In *Mirror*, significantly, the first newsreel images shown are of the Spanish Civil War refugees, who are displaced like the modern-day characters.

[5] Don't Queen have a video where Freddie Mercury releases a white dove?

[6] Translated by Andrew Jary in *Selected Poems*, Arthur Rimbaud, Crescent Moon, 2012

universal transcendence.

CHILDREN.

Andrei Tarkovsky measured his experience of childhood against that of other artists, and against commonly-held beliefs. In *Mirror* he goes back to feel again the ambiguity and pain the absent father caused (Ingmar Bergman and Steven Spielberg revisited their troubled childhoods in 1982 in movies such as *E.T.* and *Fanny and Alexander*). Tarkovsky's films act like fairy tales – mechanisms in which the unconscious expresses itself uncensored, and anguish can be powerfully expressed (a 'what if?' scenario which's allowed to run unfettered). *Mirror* works as exorcism; but it is also about the birth of the artist, and the experiences that shape the artist's life. The psychoanalyst Alice Miller wrote in *Thou Shalt Not Be Aware: Society's Betrayal of the Child*:

> Children learn about evil in its undisguised form in their early childhood and store this knowledge in their unconscious. These experiences of early childhood form the source of the adult's productive imagination... (232)

The 1975 movie shows childhood to be something essentially mysterious. The kids in *Mirror* are simply there, out in the garden, or pouring salt onto the cat's head, or running, or watching a fire. There is doing, but being takes precedence. In the Tarkovskyan childhood, everything is strange, but not necessarily threatening. There is none of that occasionally sinister and unsettling treatment of children found in American films, where children are often either sentimentalized in a cloying, cheesy manner, or they are soon to be witnesses of meaningless violence.

In Andrei Tarkovsky's cinema, children are closer to the magical, præternatural world than adults: the boy Aleksei in *Mirror* has premonitions; the bell-caster Boriska in *Andrei Roublyov* has magical gifts; in *Nostalghia* the boy asks terrifying questions in all seriousness ('is it the end of the world, Papa?'); in *The*

Sacrifice the boy Little Man sleeps in a mysterious twilit bedroom, builds houses with witches, lies like Buddha under a bo tree, and utters the divine words of Creation ('in the beginning was the Word'). Significantly, all the important Tarkovsky children, from Ivan to Little Man, are boys (except for the daughter in *Stalker*.)

In *Mirror* the familial affirmation is of the classic (archaic) matriarchal trinity: daughter, mother and grandmother (made even more personal by the director's mother, Maria Tarkovskaya, playing the grandmother, and the same actress, Margarita Terekhova, playing the wife and mother in the different time periods, and the director's wife, Larissa Tarkovskaya, playing the doctor's wife – *Mirror* was a real family movie, in every respect!).

PAINTINGS IN *MIRROR*

Using paintings as a basis for *mise-en-scène* was derided by Andrei Tarkovsky in his writings (ST, 78), although he did just that on a number of occasions in his movies. Tarkovsky used painting many times, often incorporating discussions of painters in his dialogues or visuals. There is Leonardo da Vinci in *Mirror* and *The Sacrifice*; Piero della Francesca in *Nostalghia* and *The Sacrifice*; the snowscapes referencing Pieter Brueghel in *Solaris* and *Mirror*; part of Jan van Eyck's *Ghent Altarpiece* in *Stalker*; Albrecht Dürer's *Apocalypse* in *Ivan's Childhood*; Vincent van Gogh is alluded to in the face and hands of Gorchakov; Byzantine icons appear in *Mirror*, *Andrei Roublyov* and *The Sacrifice*; and *Andrei Roublyov* has the painter's icons crowning it at the end.

Leonardo da Vinci's people – the women, angels, saints, outcasts, children and madmen – inhabit a twilit world of shadows. Some of Leonardo's subjects are half-angels, half-devils, supremely ambiguous, tantalizing, mocking and mysterious. None of Andrei Tarkovsky's people are as fully imagined as Leonardo's softly smiling angels and goddesses (as great as Tarkovsky is, I don't think he would put himself on the same level as Leonardo). It's practically impossible to portray a Leonardo face in cinema. The famous Leonardo Gioconda Smile, as enigmatic as Buddha's grin, is also unfilmable. At one point, *Mirror* tries to do it: it cuts from the *Portrait of a Woman* (Ginerva Benci?, *c*. 1474-76, National Gallery of Art, Washington, a.k.a. *The Young Woman With the Juniper*), to Natalia, the wife of the Narrator. The mythicization stems from the montage, which is bold (ST, 108).

The sitter in *The Young Woman With the Juniper* (used in *Mirror*), Andrei Tarkovsky called at once 'attractive and repellent. There is something inexpressibly beautiful about her and at the same time repulsive, fiendish' (ST, 108). Leonardo da Vinci's portrait was effective, Tarkovsky reckoned, because the viewer couldn't single out any particular aspect of the painting from the whole, it couldn't be grounded in one particular interpretation. Instead, the artwork offered up the 'interaction with infinity', an opening out into infinity (ST, 109). Easy to see how Tarkovsky might like a similar response to his own art: that the viewer wouldn't be persuaded to dissect his films, to take them apart detail by detail, but to apprehend them as a whole. It was the *whole film*, Tarkovsky asserted, that was the work of art, not any particular element. Dividing up a movie into components was to miss the point (ib., 114, 177). Only a film as a whole can carry the meanings and values that audiences ascribe to them, Tarkovsky said, not the deconstruction of individual shots or scenes.

The typical way in which painting is introduced into Andrei Tarkovsky's movies is by an actor leafing through a book (in *Ivan's Childhood*, *Mirror* and *The Sacrifice*). This may have been the way in which Tarkovsky first encountered painting – not at school or in museums, but at home, via a book, in privacy. (In a way, it's a modest, perhaps even too obvious method of weaving in a thematic subplot about painting into the films. But perhaps Tarkovsky's characters are the sort of highly educated people who might look through a book of paintings, or have such a book at home). Of all the arts, Tarkovsky folds painting and music into his cinema more than any other. He does not, for instance, make references to the history of cinema, or dance, or ballet, or musicals, or sculpture, or opera (Ingmar Bergman's films often reference theatre, for instance, while jazz (and the Marx Brothers) are never far from Woody Allen's films). Both painting and music are significantly non-verbal artforms with a tendency towards lyricism and expressionism (and they're abstract enough to fit into Tarkovsky's cinematic scheme).

Themes common to both Andrei Tarkovsky and Leonardo da Vinci include: twins, seen in Leonardo's two mysterious *Virgins of the Rocks* (c. 1483-86, Louvre, Paris, and c. 1503, National Gallery, London and other works). Twins appear in *Mirror*, and a double in *Nostalghia*. The myth of the Two Mothers – in Leonardo's beautiful *The Virgin and Child with St Anne* (c. 1510, Louvre) and the London *Cartoon* (c. 1498, National Gallery) – are found in *Nostalghia* (the Russian women in Gorchakov's dream); and in *Mirror* (the aunt and the mother). At the end of *Mirror* the matriarchal trinity is seen: the grandmother, mother and (in this case two) children, a familial configuration like that of Leonardo's *St Anne* images, where the grandmother is depicted as a Dark Mother, a Black Goddess figure.

The scene where the mother Maria flails her arms in the raining room in *Mirror* is like the modern filmic equivalent of a scene from a long lost Leonardo painting (one can imagine Leonardo – or post-Leonardoan artists like Gustav Klimt or Gustave Moreau, artists with similarly ambiguous views of women – applauding Andrei Tarkovsky for that scene. To an artist like Michelangelo Buonarroti or Gianlorenzo Bernini it would appear bemusing).

Women in Andrei Tarkovsky's cinema recall those in

Leonardo da Vinci's art – there is the same emphasis on ambiguous sexuality, fetishes (long hair), arcane gestures, prominent eyes, swan-like features, serenity, restlessness and strangeness. (Leonardo's women are the precursors of the *femme fatales* in Symbolist and *fin-de-siècle* painting, and 1940s *film noir*). It was the memory of his mother, Sigmund Freud wrote of Leonardo, 'that drove him at once to create a glorification of motherhood'.[7] The same could be said of Tarkovsky, in *Mirror*. Both artists glorify the mother: she is a gigantic figure, never fully understood by the child. She is at once dangerous and deeply desired.

The severe *Self-Portrait* by Leonardo da Vinci (*c*. 1512, Royal Library, Turin) appears in *Mirror* as the father returns to the homeland. Andrei Tarkovsky's father Arseny was a poet, an artist, and the appearance of the Leonardo sketch at this point underlines the significance of the father as a creative person, and that the film is an æsthetic construction and inquisition – in part the Story of the Birth of an Artist. The self-reflexivity of Leonardo's art is part of his mystery, and probably one of the reasons that Tarkovsky was attracted to him.

There are several still-life arrangements of props in *Mirror* which focus some of the biographical aspects of the piece (as well as drawing on the still-life motif from the history of painting). The objects include: potatoes, bread, flower petals, large glass vessels, art books (Leonardo da Vinci), jars of milk (and spilt milk). Oh, and mirrors, of course – lots and lots of mirrors!

---

7 S. Freud. *Leonardo da Vinci*, tr. A. Tyson, Penguin, London, 1965, 155.

5

MIRROR: ASPECTS OF THE PRODUCTION

THE SCRIPT

Mirror started to take shape around 1968, when Andrei Tarkovsky worked with his co-writer, Alexander Misharin (Tarkovsky had asked Misharin to help him edit the script of *Andrei Roublyov*, which Misharin had been reluctant to do, because Andrei Konchalovsky was the writer, but wasn't around at the time. Misharin helped Tarkovsky to cut out a whole section of *Andrei Roublyov*).

Andrei Tarkovsky had developed *Solaris* from early 1968 onwards (Andrei Konchalovsky was going to collaborate on the script, but the two filmmakers disagreed about the adaptation). It wasn't his first choice to follow up *Andrei Roublyov* (he wanted to make *Bright, Bright Day*, the script which became *Mirror*) and a movie about his mother (parts of this also went into *Mirror*).

Andrei Tarkovsky had originally planned filming interviews with his mother with a concealed camera, using questions such as:

'when did you begin smoking?',

'do you like animals?',

'are you superstitious?',

'are men or women stronger, do you think?',

'do you ever have friends outside your circle?',

'do you always speak the truth?',

'what would make you especially happy now?',

'have you ever envied youth?',

'which are your favourite poems?',

'are you capable of hatred?',

'which part of your life would you say was happy?',

'what do you think about space travel?',

'do you like Bach?',

'what do you remember about the war with Spain?',

'what was the funniest thing that ever happened to you?',

'are you a good swimmer?',

'do you remember the day when you sensed you would become a mother for the first time?',

'which is your favourite season?',

'have you ever starved?',

'what do you think about war?',

'what is freedom?',

'how many years did you work at the printers?',

and 'are you scared of the dark?'

The 1975 film had a number of titles. It was *The Bright, Bright Day* (or *The White, White Day*) for a long time (this title comes from one of Arseny Tarkovsky's poems). In February, 1973 Tarkovsky wrote:

> I don't like *The Bright Day* as a title. It's limp. *Martyrology* is better, only nobody knows what it means; and when they find out they won't allow it. *Redemption* is a bit flat, it smacks of Vera Panova. *Confession* is pretentious. *Why Are You Standing So Far Away?* is better, but obscure. (D, 69)

It's not just in pre-1989 Soviet Russia where filmmakers were forbidden to use a title by State institutions. In the West, titles are not copyrighted (tho' some are protected), but it would be a foolish company, however, that tried using names such as 'Disney', 'MacDonald's' or 'Coca Cola' on a product or service, those corporations being notorious for the number of litigations they pursue). But Tarkovsky is not to referring to another studio, company or artist who might prevent him from using a title, but to the Soviet authorities.

Mirror, according to the script *A Bright, Bright Day* (Mosfilm, 1973), was going to have less documentary footage and more memories of Andrei Tarkovsky's childhood. The Narrator was going to quote from Aleksandr Pushkin's 'The Prophet' (a favourite Tarkovsky text) and walk past a funeral at a cemetery, encouraging the Narrator to muse on life and death.

The *Bright, Bright Day* screenplay had opened with a scene in a cemetery, and a funeral. Scenes included the demolition of a church in 1939; the mother selling flowers in a market; a horse riding lesson; a scene at a racetrack; and a forest scene at night (M. Turovskaya, 63).

> I wanted to tell the story of the pain suffered by one man because he feels he cannot repay his family for all they have given him [Tarkovsky wrote in *Sculpting In Time*]. He feels he hasn't loved them enough, and this idea torments him and will not let him be. (133-4)

The movie would be about a mother, Andrei Tarkovsky affirmed: 'any mother capable of arousing an interest in the authors,' Tarkovsky and Alexander Misharin wrote in their proposal for *Mirror* (when the film was called *Confession*):

> as all mothers, she must have had a full and fascinating life. This must be the ordinary story of a life, with its hopes, its faith, its grief and its joys. (CS, 257)

The concept, according to Misharin and Tarkovsky, was to trace the 'spiritual organization of our society' through 'the rightful fate of one person; a person whom we know and love, who is called Mother' (CS, 258).

The Narrator in *Mirror* is strictly a *Narrator*, in the technical, literary sense of the term. Rather than being the Narrator of a novel, however, *Mirror*'s Narrator is the Narrator of poetry, because *Mirror* is a *ciné*-poem, rather than the cinematic adaptation of a novel or a play. (And, to reinforce that, *Mirror* quotes from poetry far more than novels). So, although he is heard off-screen, interacts with characters (chiefly with Natalia), and is glimpsed briefly on his death bed, he is still not really meant to be a flesh-and-blood character like Maria, Ignat or Natalia. He is the Narrator of the poem that is the film.

•

The script continually evolved, with daily rewrites (that's usual for many movies, but *Mirror* had a loose structure, which could accommodate all sorts of additions or alterations. As Andrei Tarkovsky wrote in *Sculpting In Time*, 'a great deal was finally thought out, formulated, built up, only in the course of shooting' [131]). Tarkovsky acknowledged that *Mirror* was the most complex of his films structurally and dramatically. The stuttering and hypnotism scene (which opens the film) was probably going to be put somewhere in the middle of the film, because the twelve year-old Ignat is seen turning on the television set in the present-day Moscow apartment. Ignat would thus have been introduced differently. A likely opening of *Mirror* would have been: (1) the titles followed by (2) the long tracking shot around the Narrator's apartment, establishing the present-day location, and the Narrator, then (3) the printing works scene, then (4) the mother and doctor scene in the field.

Alexander Misharin recalled that the writing process for *Mirror* had been intense for a time: he and Andrei Tarkovsky had shut themselves away for three or so weeks and wrote every day. They employed a common practice among co-writers: they wrote scenes on their own, then swapped them and edited the other's scenes. Misharin said people reckoned they knew which were the scenes Tarkovsky had written and which were his, but often the opposite was the case. *Mirror* was not only about Tarkovsky's past and family; there was plenty of Misharin's background in there, too. Misharin recalled that he and Tarkovsky only fell out seriously once or twice.

The post-production of *Mirror* was troublesome because the first rough cuts of the movie didn't work (and it wasn't simply a case of the movie-makers hating the first assembly, as they so often do. Nobody likes the rough cut of their movie).

Mirror was '*extremely difficult* to edit', Andrei

Tarkovsky confessed (my emphasis). The film, as Alexander Misharin noted, had too many scenes and too many themes, and they couldn't be arranged by editor Lyudmilla Feiginova into a form that satisfied everyone. If the scenes were arranged in a particular pattern, Misharin said, some other scenes would be left out. There was a moment of revelation when the 34 or so scenes fell into the final structure. As Misharin told it, Tarkovsky's wife Larissa had sewn a kind of sack with pockets in it, which they hung on the wall and placed the scenes in each pocket. As if by a miracle, Misharin remembered, both he and Tarkovsky had seized the scenes at the same time and shuffled them into the same order. After that, the post-production of *Mirror* continued without problems.

FILMING *MIRROR*

According to Andrei Tarkovsky's diary, *Mirror* was allocated 622,000 roubles (a small budget – about $2.5 million), and 7,500 metres of Kodak film stock (24,600 feet). Filming began in September, 1973 and finished in March, 1974. *Mirror* was not sent to the Cannes Film Festival (Tarkovsky and co-writer Alexander Misharin blamed Filip Yermash, Goskino's chairman, for this). It was released in the Soviet Union on Mch 7, 1975 at a third (then second) distribution category.

'The average Soviet feature costs about 600,000 dollars to produce, with budgets scarcely ever rising above 1 million dollars', wrote David Cook in 1990, adding, '[a]s in other Eastern European countries, both filmmakers and performers are modestly paid by Western standards' (775). The low pay of cast and crew enabled a Russian film like *Andrei Roublyov* to be produced for far less than it would have done if it had been made in the West. In the Russian system, the crew was paid a standard wage during production, having to wait (sometimes for a long time) for the bonuses.

For *Mirror*, which was filmed under schedule, the production team went to considerable lengths in the design of the piece (you had to on an Andrei Tarkovsky movie): they rebuilt Tarkovsky's childhood home, as well as re-planting the nearby field with buckwheat so that it would accord with Tarkovsky's memory of the place (ST, 132).

While making *Stalker*, Andrei Tarkovsky had problems with both his DP and set designer, both crucial roles on a Tarkovsky production. Odd, because Tarkovsky had got on with Georgy Reberg during *Mirror*, which had been one of the happier shoots for Tarkovsky; and Reberg's contribution to *Mirror* is immense. But Tarkovsky had also replaced his regular cinematographer for *Mirror*, Vadim Yusov. Even so, some of the scenes that Reberg shot – such as the waterfall scene – made it into the final cut (according to editor Lyudmilla Feiginova, DPs Reberg and Knyazhinsky and actor Aleksandr Kaidanovsky).

On *Mirror*, Andrei Tarkovsky said the crew used to visit the country house set at dawn just to experience the atmosphere of the place (ST, 106). Tarkovsky often improvized and changed his ideas for scenes as he went along (even a movie director known for rigorously sticking to the script and the storyboards, Alfred Hitchcock, in fact didn't, but incorporated new ideas and improvizations as he directed his pictures).

New ideas were written for Margarita Terekhova in *Mirror*, for instance, 'to make use of her tremendous potential' (ST, 131). She became the present-day wife of the Narrator, as well as his mother from the past (the character of Natalia wasn't in the original script). Via Terekhova came the idea for integrating the past and present scenes.

That needs to be recalled – that the actress Margarita Terekhova inspired the filmmakers to invent a new character, Natalia, and to also have Terekhova play both roles.

BLACK-AND-WHITE AND COLOUR IN *MIRROR*

Andrei Tarkovsky's use of alternating colour and black-and-white – begun in earnest with *Solaris*, but developed to the point of a major poetic trope in *Mirror* – is essentially no different from that of *The Wizard of Oz* (Victor Fleming, 1939, U.S.A.). Changing from colour to black-and-white (as in *Mirror* and *Nostalghia*) indicates a movement from one world, one mental state, one perception, to another. Sometimes the filmmakers use black-and-white to portray the past (in *Mirror* and *Nostalghia*), whereas in *Nostalghia* sepia-and-white images are part of Domenico's past and Gorchakov's Russian dreams. In a 1966 interview, Tarkovsky said he preferred black-and-white films over colour films, because black-and-white seemed closer, he asserted, to how perception works in real life, how colour isn't really noticed in real life, but colour films artificially attract attention to themselves (D, 356). Although the world is in colour, Tarkovsky reckoned that black-and-white movie somehow came closer to the psychology of art (ST, 139).

Andrei Tarkovsky's restrained use of colour produced colours that were naturalistic, muted, often optically washed-out (i.e., altered during grading or timing). Tarkovsky also liked, along with so many filmmakers, to shoot at the magic hour (some of the great magic hour movies include *The Black Stallion* (1979); one of the very best is *Days of Heaven* [Terence Malick, 1978, U.S.A.], lit by Nestor Almendros and Haskell Wexler). For *The Sacrifice*, the dawn light meant shooting at two in the morning (in May in Gotland, Sweden). The filmmakers sometimes set-dressed the natural world to achieve particular effects (such as spray painting vegetation in *Stalker*, spraying trees with water in *The Sacrifice* to make them look darker, or, for *Mirror,* painting leaves gold).

There isn't a particular scheme to the use of black-and-white, sepia and colour in *Mirror*: while other movies might employ colour for dreams and black-and-white for 'reality' (as in the most famous case, *The Wizard of Oz*), *Mirror* doesn't abide by a strict pattern. Sometimes it seems as if the different hues of black-and-white film stock in Andrei Tarkovsky's movies (as in *Mirror* or *Stalker*) was deliberate, and sometimes it appears rather arbitrary, not part of a premeditated pattern (and simply the result of how the celluloid was processed at the labs). As for the lighting, Tarkovsky favoured natural light effects, hence his interiors are often very dim (such as the houses in *Mirror* and *The Sacrifice*).

EDITING *MIRROR*

A very important person in Andrei Tarkovsky's cinema is film editor Lyudmilla Feiginova, who edited all of Tarkovsky's Russian films (she started out as assistant editor for *Ivan's Childhood*). The film editor is often a collaborator overlooked by critics, who are more likely to discuss composers, DPs, producers, or production designers, before they get to editors (if they tackle any technical stuff at all; which they rarely do).

But Lyudmilla Feiginova is hugely significant in Andrei Tarkovsky's cinema in being a major force in developing Tarkovsky's distinctive editing style. Critics of Tarkovsky's movies routinely cite the visuals, but rarely the editing. The rhythm, tempo and pace of Tarkovsky's films, though, is as central as the *mise-en-scène* or the sound. Feiginova, for example, said it was her idea to use the scene with the stutterer as the prologue to *Mirror*. This particular film went through some twenty versions before the final one was chanced upon – it was 'extremely difficult to edit', Tarkovsky recalled. (Feiginova and Tarkovsky employed a common method of laying out the film – listing the scenes on cards and shuffling them about).

•

Andrei Tarkovsky's narrative style owes something to

the stream-of-consciousness method (of the literature of James Joyce, Virginia Woolf, D.H. Lawrence and John Cowper Powys, among British novelists). *Mirror*, especially, is a sequence of thoughts, dreams, memories, newsreels and symbols. The movie was so open in form Tarkovsky admitted it was edited in twenty different ways (and no doubt, if Tarkovsky had lived on into the age of DVDs and Director's Cuts, he might have returned to editing the film: *Mirror* isn't 'finished', as no work of art is really 'finished'. Films, especially, can be reworked on so many levels in so many ways – months and months can go by. Some filmmakers, like Orson Welles, Stanley Kubrick or Francis Coppola, were famous for editing their movies up to – and beyond – the release date. George Lucas has tweaked the *Star Wars* series several times).[8] What, ultimately, fused these disparate forms of *Mirror* together was probably Tarkovsky's personal vision, his emotional commitment (and the skill and patience of editor Lyudmilla Feiginova and her assistants). The deeply psychological and poetic nature of Tarkovsky's films nevertheless means that they are very anti-psychoanalytical, non-deterministic, anti-reductionist and anti-secular in their world-view. Instead, a post-Orthodox Christian pantheism is advocated, an affirmation of the God Within, and an inkling of the emergence of a Goddess Within.

NEWSREEL.

The newsreel footage in *Mirror* is a substantial element in the 1975 movie. The newsreel footage is gathered from all sorts of sources, the result of anonymous camera teams, and from so many places – throughout Russia, but also in China, in Berlin, in Spain, in Prague, and in Hiroshima (thus, a significant proportion of *Mirror* was not directed by Andrei Tarkovsky, but was bought from film libraries).

A lot of the footage is familiar from the countless documentaries on World War Two, on Russian history, on Nazi Germany, and on 20th century history (there are

---

[8] And some *Star Wars* fans have found that very frustrating.

whole cable and satellite channels now dedicated to airing this kind of material).

But Andrei Tarkovsky and company deploy it in quite different manner from the typical TV documentary. There are no captions and no voiceovers identifying the many images and historical events. And none of the characters in *Mirror* refer to the footage, or even to the events depicted in the newsreels. Instead, *Mirror* relies on the viewer's knowledge of history to fill in the gaps. Some of the newsreels will be familiar (the nuclear bomb explosions require no gloss). But much of it will be unknown to many in the audience. At the same time, viewers will not need to know where and when some of the newsreels were captured. The remarkable footage of the Soviet balloonists, for example, or the moving images of soldiers trudging doggedly through mud and water do not require the viewer to know all the details. *Mirror* is a movie which doesn't explain everything, like the rest of Tarkovsky's output. It relies on the viewer to add their own interpretations. (Editor Lyudmilla Feiginova does employ one of the standard devices of TV news and documentaries: she and sound man Semyon Litvinov add studio sound effects to footage that was filmed silent (as a lot of it was).)

The newsreel sections of *Mirror* demonstrate that this movie takes in a huge historical sweep, from the Spanish Civil War to the Second World War and atomic bombs to Russia and China in the era of Chairman Mao.

And it works: *Mirror* can make these visual shifts from personal autobiography to big global events seem if not logical or expected, then at least poetic and emotional.

•

Andrei Tarkovsky spoke of editing in terms of rhythm, necessity, sense and unity (ST, 113-121). Each shot must be filled with time, like a glass bottle being filled up (gently but surely) by a stream of water. The aim of editing is unity – to make an organic whole out of all the parts. 'Editing brings together shots which are already filled with time, and organises the unified, living structure inherent in the film', Tarkovsky stated (ST, 114). This recalls Eisensteinian montage again. Each shot has its own 'time-pressure' (ib., 121), and these must be connected carefully.

Editing for Andrei Tarkovsky is a musical process of harmonizing and counterpointing, of refrains and codas. Editing is highly personal, the stamp of a creative personality. What Tarkovsky dislikes is the imposition of a foreign structure on the material. It should all be one – the planning, shooting, editing and post-production. The editors (Ludmila Feganova, G. Natanson, Erminia Marani, Amedeo Salfa, Nina Marcus, Olga Shevkunenko, Tatyana Yegorychyova, Erminia Marani, Amedeo Salfa, and Michal Leszcylowski) edited the movies as they were being shot, so that they could rearrange what was still to be filmed, and react to material already staged. When he moved to the Western system, Tarkovsky said he had to wait until all of *Nostalghia* was filmed before he could start editing. (Actually, most movie-makers edit as they go along, having their editors start cutting the celluloid as soon as it's been exposed).

Andrei Tarkovsky's films are open structures. They could be edited in a number of ways. Tarkovsky proves this himself, when he admits the production team got into a terrible mess over *Mirror*, which was edited into 'some twenty or more variants' (ST, 116). Indeed, *Mirror* could be re-edited *ad infinitum*. Sections could be added, subtracted, re-shuffled. Tarkovsky spoke of working very hard at editing *Zerkalo*: the twenty edited versions were not just subtly different, but were 'major alterations in the actual structure, in the order of the episodes' (ib., 116). When they tried 'one last, desperate rearrangement', the film started to gel. Understandably, it took the director a long time to believe that *Mirror* was working at last. 'For a long time I still couldn't believe the miracle' (ST, 116).

MUSIC IN *MIRROR*

Andrei Tarkovsky's main composer, Eduard Artemiev, made some restrained but evocative music for *Solaris*, *Mirror* and *Stalker*. In *Mirror*, as the camera tracks in to the condensation stain on the table there is a tumultuous crescendo in the soundtrack that sounds like Giles Swain's *Cry*, or the György Ligeti music from *2,001: A Space Odyssey*.[9] Similar music, like an orchestra all playing sustained notes at once, occurs in *Solaris*.

Eduard Artemiev said that he composed and recorded a lot of music for *Stalker*, but the Maestro concentrated on that one flute piece, using it again and again. There was also supposed to be a music cue for the tunnel (meat grinder) scene, but Andrei Tarkovsky didn't use the piece Artemiev had written (Artemiev remarked that every time he saw *Stalker*, there was a hole for him where the music should have been).

In some ways Andrei Tarkovsky's use of music is shabbier than that of Hollywood cinema. Hollywood patches up movies with awful sweeping strings and orchestras going at full speed (if everything else in a film has failed to move an audience, music is the last resort: music does so much of the emotional work in a Hollywood film. And Hollywood movies, since the 1970s, have had music cues planted throughout, as if they don't trust the audience to react in its own way to a movie, as if the audience has to be told at every stage what to think and how to feel). Tarkovsky goes even further; he selected key classical composers (J.S. Bach, Ludwig van Beethoven, Henry Purcell, Giovanni Battista Pergolesi, Claude Debussy and Richard Wagner), and chose very moving pieces of classical music: J.S. Bach's *St Matthew Passion* (in *The Sacrifice*); the opening of Bach's *St John Passion* (at the end of *Mirror*); Bach's slow, stately *Chorale Prelude in F Minor* (in *Solaris*);[10] Ludwig van Beethoven's *Ode to Joy* (in *Nostalghia*); as

---
9 Including Ligeti's *Atmospheres* and *Requiem*.
10 Plenty of Bach, then. As Jean-Luc Godard noted, Bach's music works with anything.

well as the beginning of Giuseppe Verdi's *Requiem*, with its melancholy double bass sliding ever deeper – a majestic piece of music. (Bernardo Bertolucci called Verdi mythic.)[11]

So it could be said that Andrei Tarkovsky bolsters up his movies with such powerful sounds, that he relies on music to do much of the work in his films, as much as Hollywood cinema. The ending of *Mirror*, for example, wouldn't be nearly as moving without those restless violins and clarinets and voices which chase around in the air in Johann Sebastian Bach's *St John Passion*.

---

[11] P. Kolker: *Bernardo Bertolucci*, British Film Institute, London, 1985, 61.

Japanese DVD artwork for Mirror

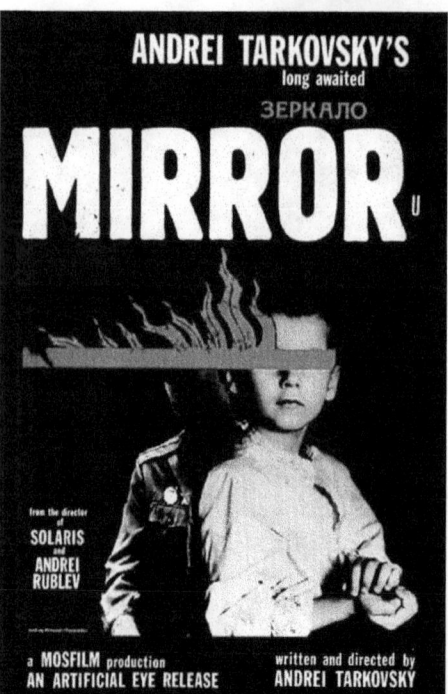

Eroticism in Mirror – Maria (Margarita Terekhova) washing her hair, and the father (Oleg Yankovsky) returns, in the levitation scene

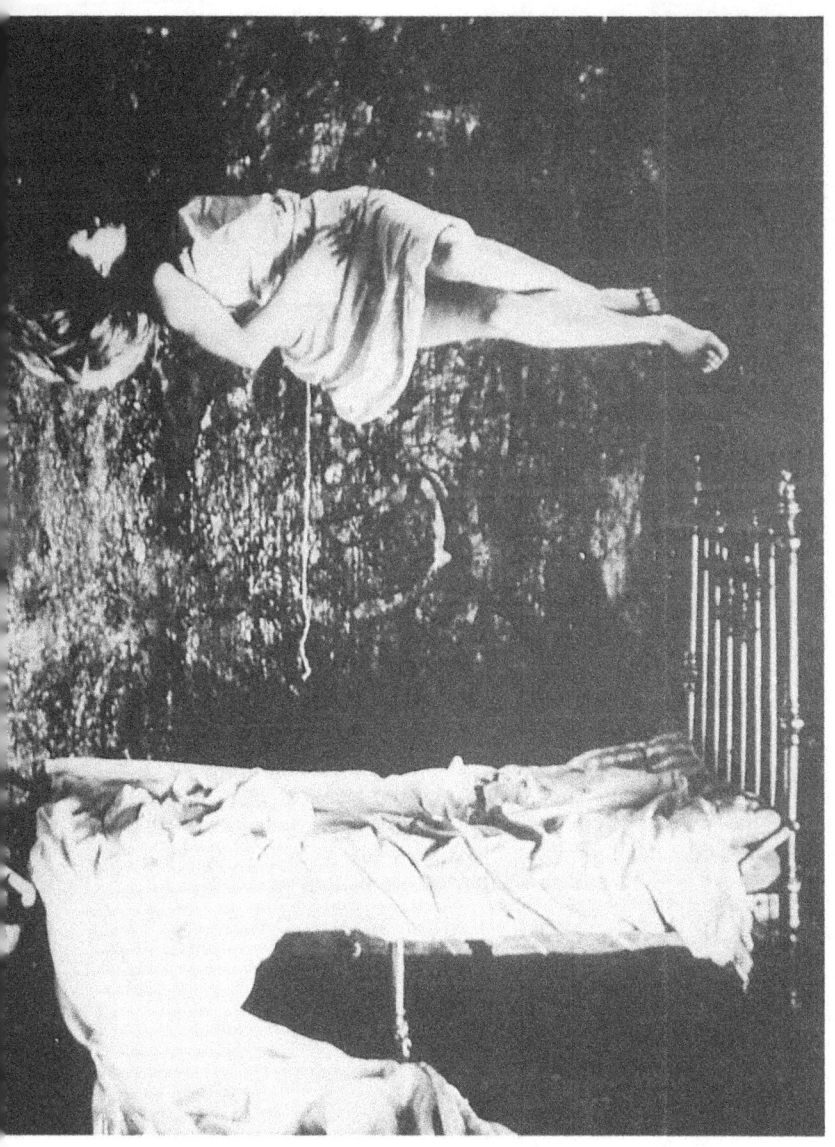

A classic Tarkovsky image: love as flying, a post-orgasmic experience of levitation. Note the metal frame bed, and the highly stylized art direction on the wall.

Stalinist Russia. Maria is rushing to the printing works (in 1935), in heavy rain. A tram and a conductor announcing stops is heard passing by. The camera, mounted high on a truck, seems to be pursuing her, as if running her down. Bleak, grey streets, rain, shabby corridors, a sparsely furnished office, bare lightbulbs.

Nikolai Grinko, Alla Demidova and Margarita Terekhova in Mirror

Mirror – a landscape out of Brueghel

A DVD cover for Mirror (below),
and Asafyev with the bird (above)

Childhood as a visionary dream – the burning barn in Mirror (above).
The fusion of three generations in the final scene of Mirror (below).

Poetic spaces in *Mirror*. The apartment scene wasn't used in the final cut.

6

MIRROR:
SCENE BY SCENE

> I think that what a person normally goes to the cinema for is time: for time lost or spent, or not yet had. He goes there for living experience; for cinema, like no other art, widens, enhances and concentrates a person's experience – and not only enhances it but makes it longer, significantly longer.
>
> Andrei Tarkovsky (ST, 63)

In the following notes on *Mirror*, the movie has been broken down into scenes, but individual shots (there are some two hundred shots) would be a better (tho' lengthier) method. Some scenes, as often in Andrei Tarkovsky's cinema, consist of only one shot. (200 shots is a very small amount for an average-length feature film; Tarkovsky reckoned 500-1,000 would be average [ST, 117]; *Nostalghia* and *The Sacrifice* are much longer, yet contain even fewer shots: between 115 and 120). By contrast, a Hollywood picture today goes to 1,500, 2,000, 2,500 or more.

Scene 1. Prologue. Documentary. (1974).

In colour, Ignat (Ignat Daniltsev) switches on the TV in his father's Moscow (modern day) apartment (we don't find out who Ignat is until much later). The TV doesn't tune in straight away. The programme shows a hypnotist/ therapist curing a shy boy's stutter, in *cinéma verité* style (the youth is a lanky teenager). There is no indication of what TV show this is, if it's a documentary, or part of some other programme. It's as if

Ignat has just switched on in the middle of a TV broadcast.

The opening of *Mirror*, with its sequence of the birth (or rebirth) of language (or access to language, or the link between language and speaking/ creation), can be seen in the terms of Lacanian psychoanalysis. In their study of Jacques Lacan in *Film Theory*, Rob Lapsley and Michael Westlake wrote:

> The entry into language and the discovery of lack in the Other therefore precipitates the child into the constitutionally unsatisfiable state of desire. In a further sense, too, the entry into language is the birth of desire. (70)

In a sense, all of *Mirror*, and much of Andrei Tarkovsky's cinema and cinema in general, concerns Lacanian *manque à etre*, the lack, the desire. The Narrator in *Mirror* goes back to the Lacanian 'mirror phase', in which his mother is the Other, as well as the mirror in which his self-idealization is reflected. So much of cinema replays the œdipal crisis of the entry into the Symbolic Order of Lacan, with its emotions of lack and desire. As Toril Moi crystallized Lacan's thought so concisely: '[t]o speak as a subject is therefore the same as to represent the existence of repressed desire'.[1]

Vida Johnson and Graham Petrie relate the stuttering boy's desire to speak to the repression of the artist in the Soviet Union (JP, 116), a familiar Western, liberal interpretation. The woman commands the teenager: 'you will speak loudly and clearly, freely and easily, unafraid of your voice and your speech'.

Much of the scene is covered in a single lengthy take, zooming out from the faces to show the two people in medium shot, then zooming back in; the shadow of the mic boom is visible. The style of the TV clip, though, has affinities with the rest of *Mirror*; there are no devices of TV (captions, voiceover, introductions) to indicate that this is a TV documentary (and it's filmed on film not video tape).

The hypnotist tries a number of devices to put the

---

[1] T. Moi, 1988, 99-100.

youth into the correct mental state (including having him lean back on her hand, which she takes away). It's familiar hypnotism stuff. Finally, she concentrates on the boy's hands, creating tension through verbal suggestions then releasing the tension in his hands and in his voice at her command. As soon as he speaks clearly, cut to:

Main titles, with organ music (Johann Sebastian Bach), white out of black (the sombre design of serious dramas).

Scene 2. The past (1935). The *dacha*.

In colour, Maria (Margarita Terekhova) sits smoking on a wooden fence between the field and the *dacha* behind her in the trees (we are presumably in the Russian countryside around the middle of the 20th century – this is confirmed in the telephone conversation we hear later, between the Narrator and his mother).

Maria wears a white embroidered dress and a black cardigan, her hair in a bun (Andrei Tarkovsky used pictures of his mother's clothes as references for Terekhova's costumes; Nelli Fomina was costume designer). She's in her thirties. The camera tracks from a wide shot up to and past Maria, from behind her; the Doctor (Anatoly Solonitsyn) is visible in the distance. The prologue is shot at the magic hour (of course). Off-screen sounds enlarge the space (a train; birds; dogs barking).

This is very much Margarita Terekhova's movie, although it's all about the director and incarnations of himself in the past, aged 5 and 12, and aged forty-four. Take away Terekhova and you have a piece that would be much less than it is, on so many levels. And Terekhova is sensational in *Mirror,* and one of the best performances in any Tarkovsky movie. Born in 1942 (so she was 31 during shooting), Terekhova is a well-known actress in Russia, but has mainly appeared in Russian productions.

The hair and make-up people (Vera Rudina did the make-up) do a fine job with Margarita Terekhova. With Andrei Tarkovsky, it's all about the hair, and in *Mirror* Terekhova's hair changes from scene to scene. An actress having her hair up or down is a simple but recurring indicator of her personality or intent in Tarkovsky's cinema. In *Mirror*, for instance, Maria as the mother has her hair up; but when her husband visits her, in the raining room scene, her hair is down. And her modern-day counterpart, Natalia, plays with her hair a lot, as does Eugenia in *Nostalghia*.

In Andrei Tarkovsky's cinema, women are exalted, exaggerated, but also denigrated and pigeon-holed. His movies limit their personalities, their potential, their sphere of action. The men always have a larger world of agency and thought, as in most other arts. The mother in *Mirror* is magnified as an Earth Goddess, a Mother-of-All. She is a working, single parent. Beyond this, her sphere of influence is limited. Although she works for a living, and is seen at work, her chief characteristic is to 'be'. *Mirror*'s modern day wife Natalia is a powerful and independent woman, who keeps the child, despite the Narrator's complaints (the Narrator in *Mirror*, Aleksei, may be Tarkovsky's most self-critical and honest portrait of a modern, 'feminized' man; but he may also be Tarkovsky's unapologetic criticism of men who were brought up – like himself – chiefly by women). Like Eugenia in *Nostalghia*, Natalia can move beyond the man. The Narrator, meanwhile, is never seen (except part of his body), but he controls the narration, the action, the whole plot of the film. The movie pivots around the mother/ wife's personality, but it is the Narrator's drive that sets the film in motion, and shapes its course (the film is his dream, his memory, his life). He's the dreamer.

The Doctor approaches. The Narrator (Innokenty Smoktunovsky), in voiceover, talks about the *dacha*, the surrounding area and his father appearing: instead the Doctor comes by (which sets up further œdipal tensions). He is a surrogate father, and wistfully flirts with Maria, knowing she lives alone. They share a cigarette. The boy (Filipp Yankovsky,[2] who is the Narrator, aged five) watches from a hammock tied between two trees, where he dozes next to his sister, Marina. (If he was asleep before, he isn't now; to emphasize that the young Aleksei is watching them, *Mirror* includes a reverse angle of Maria and the Doctor, taken from Aleksei's point-of-view). (No need to note the echoes of the voyeur of the Freudian primal scene – which is evoked again in a short while).

When the Doctor sits beside Maria on the fence, it breaks, and they both fall backwards. Maria rises quickly and dusts herself off, stepping away from the man (to establish her sense of social decorum, and her unavailable romantic state), but the Doctor remains on his back, the camera pushing in on him slowly (without cutting). The Doctor says that some living things fell with them. The Doctor, philosophical now, talks about nature, trees, bushes, plants; 'trees don't rush about, fussing... We don't trust nature anymore.' He says 'visit us' and Maria does, later, at the end of the picture (in scene 30). (The Doctor's not a nature freak, however: he mentions a hazel nut tree nearby, but Maria tells him it's an alder).

The Doctor walks away across the field, turns, and the bushes and field of buckwheat blow in the wind (Tarkovsky didn't want the actor Anatoly Solonitsyn to simply look back here, he wanted a reason for him to do so. If he had simply turned and looked back at her, it would have been false [ST, 111]). He waits a moment, as if pondering returning to Maria (the wind blows a second time, but less strongly), but he turns and leaves.

Maria turns away and goes inside the house, the camera tracking behind her, framing her against the house (the first reveal of this important setting – not only significant in the narrative, but one of the big expenses in the production). The poetry, read by Arseny Tarkovsky, begins here for the first time (the poem is

---

[2] Filipp Yankovsky was the son of the actor, Oleg Yankovsky, who played the father in *Mirror,* and the lead in *Nostalghia.*

'First Meetings' [ST, 101], which begins '[e]very moment that we were together | Was a celebration, like Epiphany'). The poem celebrates love, where the woman leads her suitor into her world 'beyond the mirror'.

This is the whole poem:

> We celebrated every moment
> Of our meetings as epiphanies,
> Just we two in all the world.
> Bolder, lighter than a bird's wing,
> You hurtled like vertigo
> Down the stairs, leading
> Through moist lilac to your realm
> Beyond the mirror.
>
> When night fell, grace was given me,
> The sanctuary gates were opened,
> Shining in the darkness
> Nakedness bowed slowly;
> Waking up, I said:
> 'God bless you!', knowing it
> To be daring: you slept,
> The lilac leaned towards you from the table
> To touch your eyelids with its universal blue,
> Those eyelids brushed with blue
> Were peaceful, and your hand was warm.
>
> And in the crystal I saw pulsing rivers,
> Smoke-wreathed hills, and glimmering seas;
> Holding in your palm that crystal sphere,
> You slumbered on the throne,
> And – God be praised! – you belonged to me.
> Awaking, you transformed
> The humdrum dictionary of humans
> Till speech was full and running over
> With resounding strength, and the word *you*
> Revealed its new meaning: it meant *king*.
> Everything in the world was different,
> Even the simplest things – the jug, the basin –
> When stratified and solid water
> Stood between us, like a guard.
>
> We were led to who knows where.
> Before us opened up, in mirage,
> Towns constructed out of wonder,
> Mint leaves spread themselves beneath our feet,
> Birds came on the journey with us,
> Fish leapt in greeting from the river,
> And the sky unfurled above...
>
> While behind us all the time went fate,

A madman brandishing a razor.

In this scene, the filmmakers have introduced a number of elements, including a scene set in the past, voiceover narrating that scene, some of the key characters, and another slab of voiceover, but a different voice, this time reciting poetry (with yet another layer of meaning added, because it is the director's father reading one of his own poems). So already *Mirror* is fairly complex, narratively. And the viewer doesn't know yet who the two Narrators are. Add to that the two spaces of the opening scenes, both set in modern-day Russia.

Scene 3. Inside the *dacha* (1935).

In colour, the mother, Maria, is filmed in glowing sunlight. She looks transfigured. The actress looks like a Madonna out of Piero della Francecsa – the eyelids are rounded, heavy, clearly defined; the round face has slightly protuberant eyes (later the actress Margarita Terekhova is deliberately compared with a Leonardo da Vinci portrait).

Outside, the aunt picks up Marina, who's half-asleep. There's a fire in a stove in the garden. A marvellous C.U. of the children sitting at the table inside with Maria combines a Tarkovskyan still-life with actors: one of the children pours salt onto a cat's head, and there's spilt milk on the table. The children seem to be whispering about some secret or game.

Maria wanders around the room, with the poetry still being read in voiceover (the poem speaks of the transfigurations of love). The camera follows her (standing in the corner, then sitting down). In another shot, the camera dollies to the open window, with Maria sitting beside it, revealing the trees and ground around the house. It's raining; there's a table below with a Tarkovskyan still-life arrangement on it; the camera tilts up to show the field beyond the trees. Dogs bark loudly, and off-screen a man's voice calls out 'Dunya!', and a woman's voice answers him ('Pasha!').

Maria goes out to see the fire, and returns to tell the children. As they run out, a complex shot follows (one of the most complex in Andrei Tarkovsky's cinema): it begins with a track and pan away from a bottle mysteriously falling off the table, to a mirror on the wall (the first of many mirrors in the movie);[3] pull focus to the boys looking at the fire; a track with another boy (identified as Klanka) who appears next to the mirror, out of the door to show the barn on fire, seen beyond a wall of rain water dripping off a gutter. The final frame is a composition in deep focus, from the rain dripping in the foreground, through the middle ground of the garden and figures, to the burning barn beyond.

A continuous shot of pure mystery: the first of many startling set-pieces in *Mirror*. It's a shot that would likely have taken an afternoon or perhaps all day to rehearse, to light and to shoot. The camera is hitting many marks, and props, actors and practical effects have to be co-ordinated with split second timing (and young child actors add further complications).

What does appear many times in Andrei Tarkovsky's *œuvre* (instead of – or despite – God) is the supernatural. 'Supernatural' is probably the wrong kind of word, being associated now with the sort of films Tarkovsky despised. But the præternatural, the miraculous or mysterious is central to Tarkovsky's sacred cinema. Doors creak open by themselves (*The Sacrifice*); objects roll around and fall to the floor (*Mirror*); or they rattle (*Stalker*); birds flap in alcoves, or burst from statues (*Nostalghia*); a bird lands on a boy's head like a blessing (*Mirror*); a bird breaks a pane of glass (*Mirror*); a lamp keeps going out and relighting itself (*Mirror*); and a candle stays miraculously alight (*Nostalghia*).

Cut to a shot of Maria against the trees; she walks to a well and drinks some water from a bucket. The camera tilts up to show the burning building (the move is

---

[3] Art director Nikolai Dvigubsky and set designer A. Merkulo must've scoured Moscow for unusual and fancy mirrors.

motivated by the man walking into frame). The creaking sound of the bucket at the well is as loud as the burning barn (an example of heightened sound fx).

Scene 4. Aleksei in bed at night (1935).

Shot 1. In black-and-white, the 5 year-old boy Aleksei (i.e., the Narrator as a child) is in a large brass bed with an ornate headboard (no sign of Marina). Near-silence, a distant bird or owl. Faint (choir?) music. Another subtle sound effect here is the clink of metal, perhaps to indicate his father's uniform.

Shot 2. Trees and bushes rustle in L.S. An owl hooting, trees blowing, a dark forest – these are primæval and timeless expressions of otherness and strangeness. Lines from Dante Alighieri are quoted in *Mirror*, where the poet spoke of being halfway through life and entering a dark forest.[4] The dark forest or *selva oscura* comes out of the *Divine Comedy*, at the start of Canto I of *The Inferno*:

> In the middle of life's path
> I found myself in a dark forest
> where the straight way was lost... (*Inferno*, I: 1-3)

Apart from Dante, *Mirror* also alludes to Aleksandr Pushkin, the *Bible*, and Fyodor Dostoievsky's *The Devils*. At the end of *Mirror*, the camera retreats into the darkened wood.

Shot 3 (as shot 1). The boy says 'Papa'. The boy gets out of bed (he's dressed in a white nightshirt), moves a chair, and walks towards his mother's room. A piece of white clothing (a shirt?) is thrown across the doorway.

---

[4] Dante's *selva oscura* or dark forest is associated, as in fairy tales, with (Christian) sin, alienation from God and error. The poet-pilgrim in the *selva oscura* is cut off from God, the 'straight way' is lost, and the task of the *Divine Comedy* is to reach the Divine Light. The hero/ heroine/ subject of both the *Vita Nuova* and the *Divina Commedia* is not God, nor the Lord of Love, nor Beatrice, nor the Virgin Mary, but the Dante-poet himself and his amazing text.

Scene 5. Maria's bedroom (1935).

The dream or memory sequence, also in black-and-white, is continuous temporally with the previous scene. The mother (Maria) and the returned father (Oleg Yankosvky) wash her hair, in a large bowl, in slow motion (the father is shown first, pouring some water). Maria is sexualized through her hair: it is often wild, in strands before her face, or wet with rain, or tied up; she often touches it and fiddles with it.

In this scene, she looks odd, her head bent down, face obscured. She stands, moves back slowly and flails her arms mysteriously. The camera pulls back too. A near-match cut shows the same room from a slightly different angle, but now empty. The walls and ceiling are dripping with water. Flames from a gas stove flicker. Lumps of wet plaster and water fall from the ceiling in slow motion, with the sound of it hitting the floor (which's wet). Eduard Artemiev's electronic music wells up. There is no local sound (and no dialogue) in this scene, but the heightened sound of water dripping, and the sound of the bits of plaster and ceiling hitting the floor.

This could relate to the Freudian primal scene – the boy's remembered glimpses of the sexual relations between his mother and father. A child's fantasy of adult sexuality, perhaps, a memory of something he never saw, but thought about (or it's the Narrator recreating it through a boy's eyes). But the room switches from the room in 1935 to a room transfigured by memory: now it's deteriorating, raining, falling apart (perhaps it's some decades later). Or perhaps the father's return disrupts the boy's psychological equilibrium, which's dramatized in this vivid fashion. Certainly the scene is abstract and ambiguous.

It's also not the *dacha* in the countryside: it's an apartment, perhaps the family's home in the Capital. The dream or fantasy or memory scene thus goes back to the time when the family was in Moscow, before the departure of the father and the move to the countryside in Summer.

Maria walks to a mirror (back to the room in 1935, but now it's still raining inside it). A lengthy C.U. of Maria follows her as she walks dreamily beside dripping walls. In a later shot, she's wrapped in a white shift and towel. Post-coital atmospheres are evoked here, as after the later cockerel-killing scene. Maria looks in the mirror, sees herself as an old woman (played by Andrei Tarkovsky's own mother, Maria Tarkovskaya, dressed similarly to the young Maria). A landscape is seen reflected in the mirror (the shot has the obscure power of a Leonardo da Vinci painting – the landscape in *The Virgin of the Rocks*, for example, or the edges of *The Adoration of the Magi*, which appeared in *The Sacrifice*). The old woman wipes the mirror, as if exploring the glassy interface between illusion and reality. The lighting changes in the middle of shots here too, to bring out the reflections in the glass and the mirrors (and adding to the theatricality). This scene ends with a colour bridging shot, a poetic refrain, of a hand warming itself on a gas flame.

In the scene, the Narrator imagines himself back in 1935, aged five, waking up to find his father returned and with his mother. The movie then leaps into the future, in a fairy tale manner, as Maria looks in the mirror and sees herself forty years later (this's the Narrator's mother Maria as she is now – in the next scene, the Narrator is talking with her on the phone). So if *Mirror* was fairly complex in terms of narration by the end of the *dacha* scenes (scenes 3 and 4), it's more complicated now, with these leaps between the past and the present, and the introduction of dream or memory sequences.

The scene also merges Maria in the past with Natalia, who we'll meet soon, in the present day: Margarita Terekhova plays both characters. The fusion of the two characters occurs in the Narrator's mind, but the film complicates the doubling effects, and keeps them mysterious. If you're trying to follow the plot or deconstruct *Mirror* as if it's a regular sort of movie, it won't work, it'll be confusing. The plotting isn't linear, doesn't follow conventional cause-and-effect storytelling, and departs from many of the usual dramatic devices of cinema.

•

There is a great deal of slow motion in Andrei Tarkovsky's cinema – mostly of the gentle kind, where actions are filmed in slight slow motion (rather than slo-mo employed in fight scenes (*The Seven Samurai, The Wild Bunch*), or action scenes (any Hong Kong action movie), or to enhance big, emotional moments (*Twilight Saga, The Lord of the Rings, Titanic*)).

In *Mirror* objects fall to the ground, people walk or run, fires flicker and the mother turns to stare into the camera in slow motion. The result is to alter perception, to re-organize reality, and take the film into another world. Often slow motion means an experience of the past, as in *Nostalghia*. But in *Mirror* slo-mo is used to re-write, and re-present, many aspects of life.

Andrei Tarkovsky's use of slow motion is not like Sam Peckinpah's films, or as it's used in horror movies – to stretch out moments of blood, guts and extreme violence, producing a cinema that is existentially visceral. Tarkovsky's slow motion is softly poetic, stemming from his lyrical view of life.

Slow motion does not, as it does in mainstream cinema, extend, elastically, some violent moment (a car crash, a bullet wound); rather, it poeticizes everyday reality. It is a lyrical device. (Slight slow motion has become far more common in Hollywood cinema, as well as TV advertizing, although the influence there comes from the speed ramping available on computers and in digital editing, and cameras which can switch film speeds within the same shot. Martin Scorsese is a particular fan of the in-camera technique, as is the *Twilight* series).

Scene 6. The present (1974), in the Narrator's Moscow apartment.

In colour, the camera pans right from some lace

curtains, which link up with the drapes in the *dacha* of the past. One very lengthy shot, tracking around the apartment, which contains: a French film poster for *Andrei Roublyov* on the wall; many mirrors; drapes half closed; plants; a sparse environment, with little furniture and few comforts (and it has the flaky, scumbled, textured walls that Tarkovsky loves, as if he's storytelling with walls). (According to Tarkovsky, people used to visit the apartment set, designed by Nikolai Dvigubsky, because it eerily recreated a sense of decay and damp).

The Moscow town apartment is a maze of mirrors, a labyrinth. Especially in the later shots of Natalia, where she is framed against a wall, there are many mirrors behind her; sometimes she stares into a mirror, playing with her hair, while conversing with the Narrator.

A telephone is heard ringing. In voiceover (presumably the man is somewhere off-camera, in the apartment), the Narrator talks with his mother about the past, about 1935, and a woman (Lisa) at the printing works who died that morning (that's why his mother is calling him). The Narrator says that he has been ill, hasn't spoken to anyone for three days, and has been dreaming about his mama as if he were a child. That line of dialogue clarifies the previous scenes for the viewer.

The conversation about Lisa and the printing works leads the spectator into the next scene. The camera continues to track towards the long dark drapes at the end of the apartment. The telephone dial tone is heard, and this sound is blended with the tram conductor in the next scene.

The first act of the Narrator in *Mirror* is to interrogate the past on the telephone to his mother. His last act, while (apparently) on his death bed, is to release a bird, a symbol since time immemorial of freedom and the soul (hinting at metempsychosis, as well as the soul flying to heaven. Whether Andrei Tarkovsky gets away with someone releasing a bird on their deathbed is another question. In an MTV pop promo it would be cheesy and silly enough to be accepted in an ironic, playful fashion, and kids in Seattle or Seoul might find it cool when their pop idol goes all arty on them, pretending to die and release a bird. But in a serious art movie it's something else: it's meant very seriously).

(In *Mirror*, in the first of the present-day scenes, at Aleksei's apartment, the camera tracks through empty rooms while Aleksei speaks to his mother on the phone. There is no indication that Aleksei is somewhere in the apartment, or where his mother is. The telephone conversation may itself be a memory. There is no insert shot of a phone either, as in the typical Hollywood movie.)

Scene 7. The past. The print works, Moscow (1935).

In black-and-white, Maria is rushing to the printing works, in heavy rain, in daytime. A tram and a conductor announcing stops is heard passing by, overlapping the previous scene. The camera, mounted high on a truck, seems to be pursuing her, as if running her down (or as if at tram height; neatly, the tram is heard but not shown, a cheap but effective way of introducing the idea of a city with trams without having to show it). The camera follows Maria in a tight long lens shot behind a fence, still tracking (these close mobile shots recur throughout the printing works scenes). Bleak, grey streets, heavy rain, shabby corridors, a sparsely furnished office, bare lightbulbs. It's Stalinist Russia.

The filmmaking has completely changed here: instead of the slow, dreamy visuals of the previous scenes, we have many mobile shots following Maria as she traverses an enormous variety of spaces in the printing works: rooms full of printing machinery, corridors, offices, areas between buildings, and more corridors. The off-screen sounds of machines are mixed high. This might be an action sequence such as a chase in a thriller movie.

Maria thinks she's made a mistake in a State (Stalinist) publication. Evocations of work in Stalin's regime in the Thirties (which relates to the opening hypnotism scene, where the youth is encouraged to speak in his own true voice, evoking freedom of speech and the freedom of the artist and the creative voice. In the Stalinist era artists were not free to say or do what they liked).

A young secretary (Tamara Reshetnikova, who's only been there a week) whimpers nervously about having a mistake in an important State document (her increasingly worried reaction is included in the scene to remind us of the potential for severe recrimination in this totalitarian administration, In the Stalinist era, people were arrested – or worse – for minor infractions, even being late for work. The scene might be Tarkovsky's criticism of the Soviet authorities of the awful treatment of fellow filmmaker Sergei Paradjanov around this time, or his own movie *Andrei Roublyov*).

The girl goes out of the office to find Lisa; Maria is searching through the papers on her desk; Lisa (Alla Demidova) enters (taller, a little older and more efficient than Maria).

The three women leave the office and head for the printing presses. Lengthy, intricate tracking shots follow Maria as she walks past the noisy printing machines to find the proofs in a cupboard (photographs of Josef Stalin and other politicos are on the walls). Her boss, the print director (played by Andrei Tarkovsky regular Nikolai Grinko) looks on wearily, and makes somewhat sarcastic moments (such as 'let some work and let others be afraid'. So he's higher up the hierarchy, and won't take the hit for the mistakes of his workers lower down the strata). (The threat and repression of the Stalin era is deftly evoked at the level of the regular worker. This is a long way from the State-endorsed cinema of Sergei Eisenstein – *Alexander Nevsky*, for instance, made in 1937).

Maria moves to a spot on her own, by the window, to examine the proofs at length. Co-workers gather around, knowing that something may be about to unfold. One of them says they've been printing throughout the night. Eventually, Maria finishes up checking the proofs.

Scene 8. Printing works.

Arseny Tarkovsky's poem "From morning on I waited yesterday" (ST, 123) is read by the poet over black-and-white tracking shots of the mother Maria as she walks along a corridor, followed by Lisa in the distance. Some of the corridor shots in the printing works are in slight slow motion (though for no obvious reason, except perhaps to enhance the unreality of this particular memory of the Narrator's mother. Andrei Tarkovsky said in *Sculpting In Time* that the slight slo-mo was employed to suggest 'a vague feeling of something strange' in the audience [ST, 110]).

This is Tarkovsky senior's poem:

I waited for you yesterday since morning,
They guessed you wouldn't come,
Do you remember the weather? Like a holiday!
I went out without a coat.

Today came, and they fixed for us
A somehow specially dismal day,
It was very late, and it was raining,
The drops cascading down the chilly branches.

No word of comfort, tears undried...

The black-and-white photography changes colour with each shot in the print works scenes – it is tinted pink, sepia, blue – created by different film stocks and processing times, perhaps.[5] Or from printing from colour film stock. Or perhaps it's intentional. (In *Stalker*, Andrei Tarkovsky stated the alterations in the hue of the black-and-white shots were intentional. Georgy Reberg, *Mirror*'s cameraman, recalled that black-and-white film stock was used to make up for the lack of colour stock; and the DP on *Solaris*, Vadim Yusov, said the same thing; which makes the use of black-and-white in Tarkovsky's movies partly the outcome of economics, not only the poetry of cinema).

---

[5] It recalls the use of tinted footage in silent cinema – blue for night scenes, for example.

Scene 9. Printing works.

Maria discusses the mistake with her colleague, Lisa, back in their office. She whispers the mistake in Lisa's ear; they laugh about it (Mark Le Fanu reckoned the misprint is 'sralin', related to the verb 'to shit', a misprint of Stalin; according to Neil Sinyard, the 'man of shit' episode caused everyone involved with the mistake to be arrested [1992, 157]). Unless the audience has foreknowledge of Soviet history, they won't have any idea what all the fuss is about. So *Mirror* withholds the reason why Maria is so upset, but when it comes to revealing it, it's whispered to Lisa. (The scene, in short, doesn't have a real dramatic pay-off – which in the repressive Stalinist Thirties might be some kind of punishment).

Maria's colleague the print director appears, bringing some alcohol (but he has little to do in this scene except to be a bystander). Maria is then severely dressed down by her fellow worker Lisa in a lengthy monologue as an over-dependent wife, selfish, with damaging emancipated ways, and is compared to Captain Lebyadkin's sister, Maria Lebiadkina, in Fyodor Dostoievsky's *The Devils,* the mysterious woman who has a small mirror, and who unmasks Nikolai Stavrogin as an usurper and pretender (the Dostoievsky reference is pure Andrei Tarkovsky).

Maria doesn't really understand the reference to Fyodor Dostoievsky, but she finds Lisa's attack disturbing, and weeps. The film concentrates attention on Maria, and the effect of Lisa's abuse, not on Lisa, or the print director, or the secretary. Big close-ups of Maria show her at her worst and most vulnerable (few Hollywood stars would accept being photographed like that).

Lisa's diatribe is over-written, too literal – and goes on for too long. The emotion isn't out of place in *Mirror*, but the length and content of the speech is.[6] At

---
[6] It has the sound of Aleksandr Misharin's writing, rather than Tarkovskys.

the end of the scene, Maria rallies, tells Lisa to grow up, and leaves the room. Lisa follows her.

Scene 10. Maria in the shower at the print works.

Maria runs ahead of Lisa, locking herself in the shower; the camera dollies along behind them (as it does a few times in these scenes), then turns about to follow Lisa as she walks off, and sings, and jumps in the air – the only bit of Gene Kelly in Andrei Tarkovsky's cinema.

In the shower, the water won't run. The shower running out emphasizes not only the harshness and poverty of the Stalinist environment,[7] but also the lack of affection and love (or understanding, or companionship) in Maria's life. The abundant water of the earlier hair-washing scene, which was aligned with Maria's sexual relations, has now run dry. Maria laughs at first, but then is downcast.

Maria is clearly depicted as someone out of touch with their time – depressed, alienated, distanced from others: an Existential outsider figure, in short (like many of Andrei Tarkovsky's characters). That she is a woman and a mother makes her far more interesting than some of Tarkovsky's other disconnected characters.

Scene 11. A connecting image.

A large fire in a field in L.S., perhaps a different, distant view of the neighbour's burning building, or perhaps another fire. A short colour shot which fades to black – signifying the end of the memory sequence.

Scene 12. The Narrator's Moscow apartment (1974).

Natalia, the Narrator's estranged wife (who's also played, like Maria/ Masha, by the excellent Margarita Terekhova), talks of her son Ignat, families and parents. She is filmed in front of a mirror (of course). The Narrator

---

[7] Where nothing works.

Aleksei, the boy's father and her ex-husband says she reminds him of his mother. Then a flashback, as an insert: Maria in the past walks away from the camera; the aunt carries the boy, outside the *dacha*. The Narrator is off-screen, as he is throughout the film (and sometimes close to the camera, so that the camera takes his point-of-view, and when Natalia talks to him she is looking into the camera).

Cut back to Natalia and the Narrator (who's also the now grown-up son of that brief insert shot) talking about repeating the same mistakes of their forebears. (Cinema can simply cut from the past to the present, and this scene is a visualization, via editing, of the concept of the 'Sins of the Fathers' influencing the subsequent generation. It is constructed, in other words, in the editing room, and the lines of dialogue about repeating mistakes help to underline the issues being explored. Off-camera dialogue can be added during editing, as new ways of cutting the movie emerge).

Scene 13. The Narrator's apartment in Moscow (1974).

Some Spanish exiles visit the Moscow apartment and talk of Spain in the old days (in colour) – bullfighting and flamenco dancing. One of the Spanish men describes a bullfight and the action of a matador. A young woman starts a flamenco dance, but is stopped abruptly by being slapped by one of the older men (presumably her father). The sound of the guitar is hastily cut, as if a record has been yanked off a record player.

The Spaniards are the guests of the Narrator (he refers to them in his conversations with Natalia). The scene acts as a meditation on being exiled in space (Spaniards in Russia), on the concept of home and the homeland, which reflects on the Narrator's exile across time, from his own memories (we are all exiles, says Juilia Kristeva). Note also how the Spaniards evoke the past nostalgically. And the film's emotional thread takes up the journey into the Spanish past with the next scene.

(You could criticize *Mirror* for stereotyping Spanish people here – what does it evoke but bull-fighting and flamenco dancing!? Oh dear).

Scene 14. First newsreel. Spain.

A montage of black-and-white newsreel, of a Spanish bullfight (with the sound of the bullring), followed by a Spanish Civil War newsreel. The footage of the Civil War is from *Native Land* (1942) a movie made by Leo Hurwitz and Paul Strand, the American photographer. The images are of human suffering (bombs, crowds, parents being separated from children, children looking lost and forlorn. The images of young children carrying suitcases are especially moving). The subtext is spiritual longing and the nostalgia of the exile, of being far from home, later explored in *Nostalghia* (that film also evoked differences in language, Italian and Russian).

Like the Spanish refugees, the Russians are also exiles (exiles in their own country – a modern, Existential version of an ancient condition). Tatiana Panshina noted that *Mirror*'s heroine 'recalls that Moses led his people out of captivity. But who will lead us, Russians, out?' (1978, 11). Hm-mmm, and where do 191 million people go? *Mirror* doesn't offer explanations for some of the suffering the Narrator and his family undergo. There are no reasons given for the breakdown of the Narrator's marriage, nor for the failure of his parents' marriage (but that's usual for an art movie, which doesn't promise or always deliver traditional dramaturgy).

•

More newsreel follows: Soviet balloonists ascending into the stratosphere – graceful images of flight, with men suspended from small balloons, and larger balloons (silence on the soundtrack at first; then choral music – is it Giovanni Battista Pergolesi's *Stabat Mater*?). Then the tickertape May Day parade of 1939. Tarkovsky said he wanted to include the footage of the balloonists simply because it was extraordinary material. And it is.

Notice how the filmmaking has changed completely again following the printing works episode: now the editing becomes very prominent in *Mirror*, with repeated cuts between the present-day scenes of the Spaniards and the newsreel footage. Another editor's ploy is used here: voiceover. It's the Narrator who is heard on top of the Spanish people talking – he's translating their words for Natalia's benefit (the voiceover thus privileges the Narrator's point-of-view).

Scene 15. The Moscow apartment (1974).

C.U. of Ignat leafing through a large picture book of paintings of the Renaissance master Leonardo da Vinci (a favourite Andrei Tarkovsky device, which introduces a different world into the film, as well as referencing some of his beloved painters): beginning with Leonardo da Vinci's *Self-Portrait* as an old man with a beard (which turns up later in the film), and also showing some of Leonardo's masterpieces: *The Virgin and Child With St Anne* (*c.* 1510), *Portrait of a Young Woman (Ginerva Benci?)* (*c.* 1474-76) and the *Mona Lisa* (1503-05), accompanied by choral music. The book is an old-fashioned art book, with tissue paper covering each illustration (only costly art books are printed like that these days. The book was a Broghaus edition which Tarkovsky knew from his childhood).

It's likely that the prologue featuring the stuttering boy would have been inserted in the scenes of Ignat in the Moscow apartment.

Scene 16. The Moscow apartment (1974).

Some time later. Natalia and Ignat sit on the floor and pick up some money when the mother drops her handbag on the floor as she prepares to go out. The boy gets a shock from one of the coins... of *deja-vu*, he says, as if he's done this before. Intimations of reincarnation here, and cyclical mythologies (as well as the physical world not being the limits of the world, a recurring theme in Tarkovsky's *œuvre*). It's also a rather clumsy piece of dramaturgy in sustaining the nostalgia and memory theme.

Natalia, before she leaves, says his grandmother, Maria Nikolayevna, might call at the apartment. Andrei Tarkovsky said (in 1985) that even he wasn't sure why the mother at the door thinks she's got the wrong place (it wasn't explained in the script, either, and it was too late for Tarkovsky to invent a subplot explaining it).

Scene 17. The Moscow apartment (1974).

Some time later the same day (in colour). Ignat is left alone by Maria. The boy has a visitor in a semi-dream or memory sequence (or he is transported back in time), after moving from the front door: a severe-looking Spanish woman (Tamara Ogorodnikova), sitting in an adjacent room in the apartment, is being served tea by a maid; she commands Ignat to find a particular notebook. Ignat obliges by finding the book on the nearby shelves. Ignat starts reading aloud from Jean-Jacques Rousseau, but the woman asks him to find another passage. Ignat reads aloud from Aleksandr Pushkin's 1836 letter to Piotr Yakovlevich Chadayev about the Christian schism that helped form Russia. Russia here is described as a buffer between the Christian West and the Mongol East.

The Spanish woman doesn't introduce herself, and isn't named; and she wasn't one of the group of Spaniards who were in the apartment earlier. (The Spanish lady was interpreted as the poet Anna Akhmatova by some viewers. Tarkovsky said it wasn't, but she was played by Tarkovsky's production manager, Tamara Ogorodnikova. And the confusions multiply, because Ogorodnikova also plays the aunt in the 1930s scenes, *and* an unnamed friend or neighbour of the family in the 1970s scenes).

She commands the boy to go to the front door. Ignat's grandmother (played by Andrei Tarkovsky's real mother, Maria Tarkovskaya) is there, but thinks she's got the wrong apartment and moves away. A bizarre occurrence, because she must have been to the apartment many times (the scene also fuses the time travel aspects of this part of the movie, the Spanish woman from the past connecting with what's happening outside the apartment in the present). Tarkovsky acknowledged that this scene was not successful, but was created to convey the confusion and shyness of the old woman.

Ignat turns back, and finds that the Spanish woman and her maid have disappeared, along with the tea cup. Slowly the camera pushes in to the table: the music, the original score (by Eduard Artemiev), wells up to a crescendo of impossibility: the boy has had a phantom visitor, yet her cup has left a condensation mark on the table, which gradually disappears.

At the end of the scene, Ignat's father (the Narrator) calls him on the telephone, asks if his mother called, and mentions a red-haired girl from the past he once desired, which leads neatly into the following scene.

•

Throughout the phantom visit from the Spanish woman and her maid, Ignat acts at first surprised to see them, though not particularly afraid. This's no Hollywood horror flick, no Stephen King or Clive Barker outing, where many another twelve year-old kid would be freaked out if these two figures suddenly materialized out of nowhere in the otherwise empty apartment. Ignat doesn't spend any time trying to work out how they got there, either; he is no ghosthunter or supernatural detective. This isn't *Ghostbusters* (1984), *The Goonies* (1985), *The Ninth Gate* (1999) or *Van Helsing* (2004).

However, some of the dramatic devices of horror or suspense movies are deployed here – the recurring music cues from Eduard Artemyiev, for example, and how those ominous, electronic drones are integrated into the flow of images.

This is one of the forms of filmmaking that Andrei Tarkovsky often used – strange sounds, unusual images, to evoke the supernatural, or simply experiencing the world at an odd angle.

Finally, the *impetus* for the visit doesn't seem to come

from Ignat, but from his father, the Narrator. The film is really about the Narrator and his memories and dreams, not about Ignat. But Ignat is, if not the catalyst, sometimes the vehicle or carrier or observer of the Narrator's life and memories. He experiences parts of his father's memories (again, without explanation in the film).

Some of the dreams in *Mirror* are anxious: the boy wandering alone in the *dacha* in the later memories or dreams, for instance, with his mother distant or behind a locked door, are not comforting evocations of the maternal realm of the past. The memory of the return of the father from the war is not particularly warm, either, and neither is the flashback of Maria at the printing works.

It isn't explained exactly who the Spanish woman is, nor why she is there, nor her relation to Ignat or the Narrator. The group of Spanish exiles, too, might be guests of the Narrator, but might not be (Natalia, his estranged wife, interacts with them, but the Narrator does not; like Gatsby, he is always elsewhere, and especially at his own gatherings). But if the viewer recognizes that the movie is really interweaving big historical events with the personal lives of the characters, from the past (1930s and 40s) and the present (1970s), it makes sense. But *Mirror* introduces such elements at first without signalling their precise function within the whole film; Andrei Tarkovsky and his team steer the film back and forth through time, and between the local and personal and the historical and political, without always clearly marking each transition (further layers are heaped up with dream and memory sequences). It is simply assumed that the viewer will be able to keep up.

Scene 18. Practice gun range. The past (1942-43).

In the Russian countryside in the snow, in colour. This is a memory sequence of the father's childhood (but the Narrator is not at the centre of this particular section), which follows on from his telephone call in the previous scene (although the Narrator is now some seven years older). The redhead girl with the chapped lip (Olga Kizilova) that the Narrator/ father desired, is seen (she remains a mysterious, elusive object of adoration, smiling shyly like the Mona Lisa, and she doesn't have a line of dialogue). The long hair, the chapped lip, the shy smile, the long skirt, the snow – it's classic Tarkovskyan eroticism.

A Leningrad orphan,[8] Asafyev (Yuri Sventikov), is the focus of this sequence: he weeps when commanded to about turn by a wounded veteran officer (Yuriy Nazarov); Asafyev takes him literally and turns through 360°, facing the other way from his cohorts. The officer berates him. The youths stand around in the snow at the end of the shooting range in the daytime.

Another boy terrifies the group of would-be soldiers when a practice grenade is picked up and then thrown (it was Asafyev who produced the grenade from his bag). The officer hurls himself on top of the grenade which rolls down the shooting range, to protect the boys. The camera tracks in to the man and a heartbeat is heard on the soundtrack. Time is stretched out – the explosion of the grenade is expected, but doesn't happen.

In a slow tilt-up shot from the prone officer to the youths in the distance, one of them says it was only a practice grenade. The veteran soldier wearily gets up and sits on a stool, in a C.U. follow shot. The red-haired girl is seen again, touching a cold sore on her mouth (chapped or sore lips are a recurring motif in Andrei Tarkovsky's child characters, and nose bleeds are frequent, too. In Japanese cinema and *anime,* nosebleeds are a stand-in for sexual repression and arousal).

This scene is not straightforward, either. For a start, Aleksei (the Narrator) at age twelve is played by the same actor (Ignat Daniltsev), who is the Narrator's son Ignat. So the same actor plays both the Narrator at age 12 and the Narrator's son (who also happens to be 12). But that's not the only complicated thing about this scene:

---
[8] One of the other kids remarks that Asafyev has lost his parents recently.

although the scene is the *Narrator's* memory, it actually features the boy Asafyev more than the Narrator (which's also true of the following few scenes). So Asafyev is another stand-in or equivalent for the Narrator. In which case, these memories are not so much personal ones of the Narrator, but more generic ones, of kids growing up at this particular time and in this particular place. But the film moves into a big historical framework when it intercuts these scenes in the snow at and near the shooting range with more newsreel footage.

The filmmaking is dynamic, too: many of the beats within the scenes are staged using lengthy takes, with the camera reframing and refocussing several times. The camera is either close to the actors, or captures them with long lenses. Although the action may be somewhat static (actors standing about or walking slowly), the interplay of the camera with the actors is vigorous, emphasizing an emotional, psychological flow between the characters and in the dialogue between the present and the past.

Paintings by Pieter Brueghel which inspired Mirror

Arseny Tarkovsky

Poster for Andrei Roublyov

Leonardo's self-portrait, used in Mirror

Leonardo's immortal faces: the portrait of Ginevra Benci, used in *Mirror*.

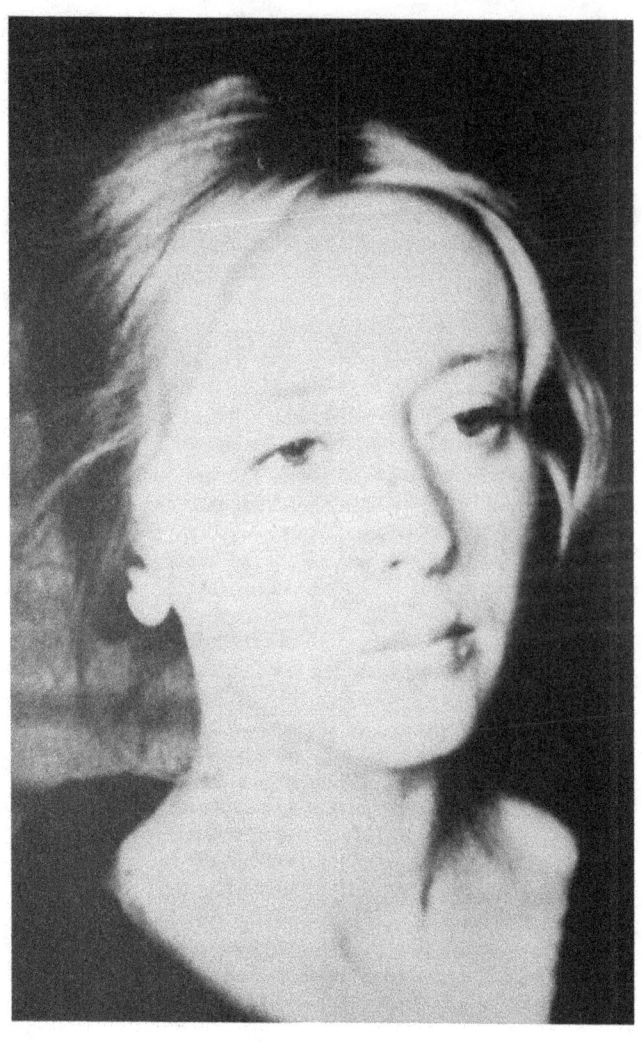

Margarita Terekhova in *Mirror* – one of the great close-ups in cinema

Scene 19. Newsreel. Crimea, 1943.

Then follows a complex montage of cross-cutting: between the memory sequence in the snow of 1942-43 (the personal) and newsreel images (the political and social): Soviet troops crossing Lake Sivash in the Crimea, 1943, with overdubbed local sound, in black-and-white – first water noises, ominous drumbeats, then troops wading through water, with Andrei Tarkovsky's father's poetry read over the images towards the end of the sequence (the poem is 'Life, Life', one of Tarkovsky senior's signature pieces [ST, 143]). The shallow, muddy lake recalls the flooded forest of Tarkovsky's other World War Two movie, *Ivan's Childhood*.

Andrei Tarkovsky recalled that the footage of the people dragging themselves through the mud had a 'piercing, aching poignancy' (ST, 131). Apparently, only a few survived the ordeal, and the cameraman was killed the same day (ibid.).[1]

This is the whole of the poem 'Life, Life':

1
    I don't believe in omens or fear
    Forebodings. I flee from neither slander
    Nor from poison. Death does not exist.
    Everyone's immortal. Everything is too.
    No point in fearing death at seventeen,
    Or seventy. There's only here and now, and light;
    Neither death, nor darkness, exists.
    We're all already on the seashore;
    I'm one of those who'll be hauling in the nets
    When a shoal of immortality swims by.

2
    If you live in a house – the house will not fall.
    I'll summon any of the centuries,
    Then enter one and build a house in it.
    That's why your children and your wives
    Sit with me at one table, –
    The same for ancestor and grandson:
    The future is being accomplished now,
    If I raise my hand a little,
    All five beams of light will stay with you.
    Each day I used my collar bones
    For shoring up the past, as though with timber,
    I measured time with geodetic chains

---

[1] Mark Le Fanu remarked on the beauty and refulgence of the images which *Mirror* introduced (rightly) without explanation. 'The sequence is as close as possible in Tarkovsky's work to absolute cinema' (77).

        And marched across it, as though it were the Urals.

3   I tailored the age to fit me.
        We walked to the south, raising dust above the steppe;
        The tall weeds fumed; the grasshopper danced,
        Touching its antenna to the horse-shoes – and it
                                prophesied,
        Threatening me with destruction, like a monk.
        I strapped my fate to the saddle;
        And even now, in these coming times,
        I stand up in the stirrups like a child.

        I'm satisfied with deathlessness,
        For my blood to flow from age to age.
        Yet for a corner whose warmth I could rely on
        I'd willingly have given all my life,
        Whenever her flying needle
        Tugged me, like a thread, around the globe.

So this is complex, narratively, combining: memory sequences (or extended flashbacks), newsreel footage unconnected directly with the memories, plus a voiceover of poetry. In addition, the under-score from Eduard Artemiev is sometimes emphasizing the lyricism of the images, and sometimes providing menacing, percussive sounds.

Scene 20. A hillside in the snow (1942-43).

Same space and time as Scene 18 (but a while later). A Pieter Brueghel *mise-en-scène* in colour (his 1565 painting of *Winter*): people sledging, other figures dotted about the snowscape. A lakeside. The boy, Asafyev, walks up the hill towards the camera, into a big close-up. He is weeping, but also whistling. It's a touching portrait of an orphan, the exile from the city: he's already the outsider, already alone in amongst all those people on the hillside.

Anonymous figures are dotted about the snowscape with a similar meticulous sense of *mise-en-scène* that informs *Last Year At Marienbad* (Alain Resnais, 1961, France). And in *Solaris* Kelvin and Hari contemplate one of Pieter Brueghel's paintings of peasants at play in the snow (*Hunters In the Snow*, 1565, Kunsthistorisches

Museum, Vienna). The camera pans around the many details of the painting in *Solaris*, to the stately sounds of Johann Sebastian Bach. This is a long sequence: at the end of it, there is an insert of a boy and a swing in the snow. This is from Kelvin's father's home movie. Later, Kelvin replays this film, in which his mother appears.

Olivier Assays said that Pieter Brueghel's *Winter* 'reproduced' in *Mirror* gave him

> a very powerful reaction, which had to with a certain way of looking at nature, when winter has reduced it to a state of pure transparency, to its essence; in winter there is a sort of simplification, translucency of the world, the light is more transparent, the cold renders our perceptions more acute. (1997, 25)

It was limiting, Andrei Tarkovsky reckoned, to employ the techniques and devices of older artforms in cinema, such as painting or theatre. For a filmmaker who so often referred to paintings, and created images from paintings, Tarkovsky was also suspicious of using too much from the history and theory of painting, which could make cinema too derivative (ST, 22). It could be that here he is saying no more than 'I remember childhood Winters as if they were from a Brueghel painting.' Maybe. Maybe all Winter snow scenes *should* look like a Pieter Brueghel painting.

Scene 21. Newsreel. World War Two, 1945.

Black-and-white newsreel, consisting of:

(1) Soviet troops in Prague in 1945;

(2) a Moscow victory parade, with fireworks;

(3) people on crutches;

(4) bombs and air raids, accompanied by loud explosions;

(5) an atomic bomb, with a loud electronic cue;

(6) another atomic bomb (which looks like a nuclear test on an ocean atoll).

All these images from the Second World War (mainly 1945), and just after, are accompanied by timpani and symphonic cues which encourage the viewer to perceive the newsreel as momentous, dangerous.

Scene 22. Hillside (1942-43).

As Scene 18. Asafyev on top of the snowbound hill in M.C.U.: he looks into the camera, as if contemplating the scenes that the viewer has just witnessed, then walks away a little; a bird lands on his head. There are three tiny ellipses in this shot, to shorten it in the editing (Asafyev's briefcase moves slightly, as do the figures in the background). He reaches up and holds the bird. It's one of those sequences in an Andrei Tarkovsky movie which sound dumb on paper, but make sense when you see them. It's magical, but not cute or sentimental (Asafyev's solemn expression steers it away from something Disneyesque).

Scene 23. Newsreel. China, 1959.

Black-and-white footage of China, 1959. Maoism. Crowds with the *Red Book*, pictures of Mao Zedong, a vast Chinese demonstration (Damansk Island in 1959). One can see how big *Mirror* is as a narrative in its scope, how it can leap from quiet, intimate moments, like Asafyev with the bird in the snow, to China and Maoism in the late 1950s. Andrei Tarkovsky and editor Lyudmilla Feiginova developed a structure and cutting pattern that could accommodate such immense leaps across space and time.

Scene 24. The past and present mixed together (1942-43 and 1974).

Shot 1. In the modern-day, Moscow apartment, Natalia is cutting wood on the floor. She looks up. The Narrator, off-camera but within her eye-line, addresses her, and says, 'what about the children?'

Shot 2. Aleksei's father, looking down, dressed in a soldier's uniform, in the past (1943), returned from the war. He's standing near the house in daytime, and looking down, as if at Natalia in the present day. (An eyeline match, in other words, that arches across thirty years).

Shot 3. The two children, brother and sister (Ignat and Marina), now aged 12 and about 10 (i.e., in 1942-43), talking in the woodland, near the *dacha*. Their father calls them from a distance (off-screen). (It's another Return of the Father sequence, echoing the one earlier). The camera tracks into the girl from behind, who's crying.

Shot 4. L.S. of the two kids. Their father calls them again. They run. The camera tilts down to Leonardo da Vinci's *Self-Portrait* (*c*. 1512) in the large picture book on a table (which Ignat had been looking at).

Shot 5. L.S. of children running towards the camera (Ignat trips over, which appears to be a mistake that was left in).

Shot 6. Natalia, in the present day Moscow apartment, thinking, as if looking at the scene in the past.

Shot 7. The 1942-43 past again: C.U. of the father embracing the children. Operatic music (J.S. Bach) comes in loudly, singing of the Resurrection and the veil of the temple being rent from top to bottom. Ignat hides his face in his father's chest, as if cowering from the loud music.

Shot 8. Leonardoi da Vinci's *Portrait of a Woman (Ginerva Benci?)* (*c*. 1474-76), with a bright light reflected on it. Andrei Tarkovsky said the painting was used as a 'timeless element' cut into the flow of moments in *Mirror* (ST, 108).

Shot 9. In black-and-white, Natalia, deliberately juxtaposed with the Leonardo da Vinci image, talks to the Narrator (who remains off-screen, as usual). Natalia is lit harshly from the side. There are two tall mirrors against the wall. This is a present-time echo of the scene from the past – the father returning to see the children. They discuss parental rights, who should have the child, and marital relations. The families of then and now are compared. The father/ Narrator is repeating the mistakes his own father, the soldier, made (once again illustrating the theme of the Sins of the Fathers).

Ignat walks into frame, and the camera pans left to follow him. The Narrator/ father asks Ignat if he'd like to come live with him and Ignat looks very surprised, and says, no, there's no need. Natalia also showed surprise a moment earlier that her ex-husband would suggest that. At the end of the shot, the camera zooms into a mirror.

Cut to Ignat wandering in the apartment, on his own (and still in black-and-white). The Narrator/ father and Natalia are heard in voiceover.

During this scene, Natalia is looking at some large black-and-white photographs, which include Aleksei's mother. Natalia comments that she does look like Aleksei's mother (not surprising, since the same actress also played Maria). In the photo, the actress Margarita Terekhova is wearing the mother's dress of forty years ago.

The scenes of the Narrator and his estranged wife arguing are the bitterest in Andrei Tarkovsky's cinema. The arguments about their son, their relationship, his mother, and her possible marriage, are full of guilt and regret. The Narrator bitchily gripes about Natalia's new relationship (with a wannabe writer), while Natalia wonders what the hell she ever saw in this self-hating, misanthropic man.

Scene 25. The Moscow apartment (1974).

Natalia is framed in C.U. against a mass of books as she is interrogated by the Narrator (and listens while the Narrator talks about himself). She is lit from below (the kind of harsh lighting a Hollywood star would hate). In the same lengthy shot, she walks slowly next to two mirrors, and leans against one; she moves into a brightly lit spot, then into shadow; then she's framed against a window, playing with her hair; it's raining outside (it's always raining in *Mirror*); the camera tracks to Ignat outside, who's burning a bush in the courtyard.

This is a very lengthy take (the longest shot in the 1975 film, at 3 minutes 55 seconds). The shot refuses the reverse angle, of the Narrator, who is presumably standing nearby, as he's able to see Ignat outside, and Natalia seems to be looking at him. Instead, the focus is on actress Margarita Terekhova. She really is superb in *Mirror*, expressing so much about her relationship with the Narrator (so there isn't a need for the reverse angle to reveal him).

Some of the dialogue is about Ignat, and what to do with him. Some of it has the Narrator belittling Natalia's choice of a replacement for him. Natalia's weary responses demonstrate that she's heard all of this before from her ex-husband, the Narrator. She asks how he got to be so miserable.

The movement of Natalia, leaning on the wall or moving slowly along it, from right to left, recalls the shot and motion of Maria in the raining room, in the earlier memory scenes. Natalia leans down and her hair is seen, as before, like Maria's. An abrupt cut to:

Scene 26. The past. Around the *dacha* (1935-36).

A linking shot of the trees in the past at night, darker than before, in black-and-white (the imagery of the scene (scene 4) where the five year-old Aleksei climbs out of bed).

Scene 27. The past (1935-36). The *dacha*.

Interior of the old house in the countryside outside Moscow (now in colour), with the Narrator's voiceover but no local sound (the Narrator speaks about the cherished spaces of his grandfather's house, and how he is dreaming of the past). The Narrator's memories are shown here: the boy (the Narrator as a child) sits on a bed on the floor; Marina plays with water by the door, beside a large glass vessel, another shot with fire (he lights a match in darkness). Maria moves through the *dacha* in a white summer dress. A big vase of flowers is on the table.

The action is covered in a complex sequence shot which has many moves and beats (it's a reprise of the shot in the first act, and was likely filmed around the same time in the schedule).

Scene 28. The past (1935-36). Around the *dacha*.

The five year-old Aleksei is outside the house in the trees, in black-and-white. A zoom into the house. The boy is at the door. Slow, eerie music.

V. Johnson and G. Petrie suggest that this black-and-white sequence is the Narrator's dream of not being able to re-enter the house (JP, 127).

Scene 29. The past (1935-36).

Shot 1. The boy says 'Mama!'. In black-and-white, the boy is seen at the door, outside the house. The door opens by itself, mysteriously.

Shot 2. A pane of glass falls out of a window in slow motion: a bird (a cockerel?) breaks it.

Shot 3. The trees again, but by daylight. A fierce wind blows them: track left to a low table, with objects such as apples, bread, a spoon and a glass vessel on it. Some of these items fall off the table in slow motion (another take of this shot occurs later on).

Shot 4. House and trees, in slow motion: the boy runs into the house. Leaves fall from above.

Shot 5. Aleksei moves past some washing, blowing in the breeze and goes to the door. He tries it; it's locked. He comes back, out of frame. The door opens. The mother is crouched behind the door, staring off-camera, as if at the boy, picking up some potatoes, in slight slow motion; behind her rain is seen through a window (but it's not raining in her doorway). A dog pads out of the house.

This scene collages images of Aleksei age five and the *dacha*, the shots made more mysterious and ambiguous by the slight slow motion. The sequence has the unreality of a dream, as if the Narrator of 1974 (aged 44) is trying unsuccessfully to rebuild a fragmented memory of 1935 (when he was five). It's as if he can remember the spaces of the house clearly, and that his mother was there, but not the exact emotion of the moment, nor what people were actually doing.

Scene 30. The past (1942-43). The Doctor's house.

In colour now, Aleksei (aged 12) and his mother Maria visit the Doctor's house (the Doctor, significantly, is absent – as is Aleksei's sister Marina, from this and the following scenes, though no explanation is given. However, the emphasis has always been on Aleksei in *Mirror*, reflecting the bias of the biographical exploration from director Andrei Tarkovsky).

It is dusk, near a river. The boy walks in bare, muddy feet. After some hesitation, and awkward talk with the Doctor's wife (played by Andrei Tarkovsky's second wife, Larissa Tarkovskaya, who was also the assistant director for *Mirror*), the two are eventually invited in to the house (class barriers are emphasized – Maria is polite and deferential, at first at least). No music in this part of the movie, but the sounds of water dripping. (The house is a predominantly wooden structure, lit by yellowy light; lamps; old wooden furniture; rain drips over the front door, as usual. The Doctor's wife wears a silky, elegant, damson dress which's meant to look out of place. And it does: the wife is depicted as a self-centred and vain woman, who never stops admiring herself with the earrings in mirrors – every interior in *Mirror* boasts a substantial quantity of looking glasses).

While the two women talk in an adjoining room about the earrings Maria's brought to sell for food, Aleksei starts to dream. The light changes. String music comes in (Henry Purcell, from the opera *The Indian Queen*, 1695). A slow zoom in to a C.U. of Aleksei's face looking at himself, reflected in an elliptical mirror; a reverse angle follows.

A succession of odd images: a C.U. of milk dripping onto the floor; an oil lamp that keeps going out and relighting itself.

Three different fires are seen, in succession: a woman, not Maria but the boy's father's one-time girlfriend, the red-haired girl with the chapped lip, is sitting next to one fire and warming herself. The man in the scene is not Aleksei's father, but the military officer, who also loved the girl. Aleksei seems to be having visions of the instructor's sexual relations (and perhaps his father's). There are echoes also of his father's relationship with his mother, because the hand seen warming itself on the flame is in, apparently, the parents' bedroom or a similar room (an image from the erotic raining room sequence in scene 5). And a mirror in a wardrobe.

The hand in front of the fire in *Mirror* acts as a motif connecting the past, memories and the present; it recalls a similar motif in *Hiroshima Mon Amour* (Alain Resnais, 1959): there is a shot in *Hiroshima Mon Amour* of the Japanese lover's hand followed by an image of the hand of her previous (German) lover.

Aleksei stares at himself in the oval mirror, in a slow zoom. This could be a dream within a dream (i.e., the Narrator in the present is remembering himself in the past having a dream, and perhaps a dream within *that* dream).

Cut to: the two women next door, in C.U., talking, with the sound of water dripping. The Doctor's wife is trying on the earrings. She comes in to find Ignat sitting in the dark; she relights the lamp. (The woman looking into the mirror at the earrings Tarkovsky thought was the kind of shot Ingmar Bergman might have done.)

Scene 31. The neighbour's house again, in the past (1942-43).

A continuation of the previous scene (in colour). The mother and son are shown the woman's child in another room; a slow zoom into the sleeping child. The Doctor's wife talks over reaction shots of Maria and C.U.s of the baby. A low, mysterious music cue.

The child is clad all in white, in a luxurious cot with a white canopy and white sheets, like a vision of Christ in the manger. Perhaps this is an alternative life or the future as it could have been, for Aleksei, to have a wildly affectionate mother. His own mother, Maria, is not affectionate – or at least not physically. Mother, son and daughter very seldom (if ever) touch. Throughout the scene Maria's poverty and emotional aloofness is contrasted with the Doctor's wife's comparable luxury and demonstrative affection (for such a revered figure, *Mirror*'s chief mother figure is surprisingly unmotherly).

The scene evokes ovulation, wombs, pregnancy, nurturing (the Doctor's wife says she is in her fourth month, and wants a daughter this time), and intense, overwhelming maternal love (the house as a womb, the imagery of fires and warmth, the daydreaming, the milk). But also a smug, indulgent, vain, proto-bourgeois form of domesticity and maternity. Maria reacts by wanting to leave quickly, and says she feels sick.

Scene 32. The Doctor's house (1942-43).

The cockerel killing sequence (in colour). The Doctor's wife persuades Maria to do it (with an axe, on a log), as she feels nauseous, being pregnant. Maria sits against a wooden wall, lit from below.

The bird is killed off-screen, but some feathers flutter around the Doctor's wife in C.U. After Maria's dispatched the bird, water runs down the walls; she lifts her head, stares into the camera and smiles, her face lit luridly (and unflatteringly), from below. It looks like the most fun Maria's had for some time.

Cut to: the father, filmed in black-and-white and slow motion, staring straight at the camera, and, by implication, at Maria (it's a match cut, along the eyeline). He turns, and strokes a woman's hand as the camera zooms out (accompanied by Johann Sebastian Bach on the track). Maria is apparently ill and floating above a bed; she wears a white cotton dress.[2] She says 'it's as though I'm floating in the air.'

This could be Maria's dream of her former sexual life with her (estranged) husband, as well as the Narrator's memories or imagined evocations of his mother's and father's sexual relations. (The link with Maria's erotic experience with her husband is reinforced by the rain running down the wall behind her, a refrain of the 'raining room' scene earlier in the film).[3] The scene certainly illustrates the height of the love between Ignat's parents, so it may be a vision of an erotic union which produced a child – the Narrator.

The erotic components of the scene are unusually explicit in Andrei Tarkovsky's cinema (sex and death are bluntly brought together, with the cut from the cockerel killing to the orgasmic floating above the bed. The additional symbolism of blood, sacrifice, ritual, cockerels, beheading and all the rest don't need any glossing).

Cut back to the Doctor's house: Maria and Aleksei swiftly take their leave of the neighbour, without waiting to be paid for the earrings.

Scene 33. A riverbank in the past (1942-43).

Maria and her son walk beside a river, coming back from the earring and cockerel scene, in a dollying two shot. Maria, smoking and thinking, moves into M.C.U. Poetry is read over this scene (there's no local sound); the poem is 'Eurydice' (by Daddy Tarkovsky), which contains images of birds, fire, souls, skies and freedom. This is the whole poem 'Eurydice':

A person has one
Body, like a solitary.
The soul is repelled
By the unbroken casing
With its ears, and eyes

---

[2] Many other European film directors of the early Seventies would've had Maria naked.

[3] Olivier Assays suggested that this scene depicted the conception of the filmmaker (1997, 24). Sure, why not? Everyone has to be conceived some time.

The size of a coin
And, dressing the skeleton,
Scar upon scar of the skin.

The soul flies through the eye
Into the heavenly brook,
On to an icy cogwheel
Of a bird's chariot
And it hears through the bars
Of its living prison
The rattle of forests and cornfields,
The trump of the seven seas.

The soul is sinful without the body,
Like the body without a night-shirt, –
No thought or deed,
Design or line.
Here's a riddle without a solution:
Who will return
Having danced on the platform
Where nobody dances?

And I dream of another
Soul, differently clothed:
It burns, as it passes
From shyness to hope,
It encircles the earth,
In liquid fire, without shadow,
Like the cluster of lilac
Left on the table.
Run, my child, don't lament
Over poor Eurydice;
Drive your copper hoop
With a stick round the world,
While in answer to each step –
Even though you don't hear it –
Both happy and dry
The earth sounds in your ears.

Scene 34. The trees around the *dacha*.

The trees and bushes again, in black-and-white and slow motion (similar to shot 3 in scene 29). The camera tracks left to a table with bread and a lamp on it. No sound of the wind, just the poetry in voiceover.

Scene 35. The house in the past (1935-36).

In slow motion and black-and-white Aleksei enters

the now deserted house (it's a continuation of scene 29). Giant spherical bottles of water are on the table (another Tarkovskyan still-life motif). The camera pans left. The poetry voiceover stops, and there is a strange sound of wind. The room is filled with hangings and clothes on lines, veils and lace drapes, blowing in the breeze. The windows are open. This image is spectral, very lyrical (and Felliniesque – recalling the memories of the film director Guido Anselmi (Marcello Mastroianni) in *8 1/2*). The camera becomes the wandering spirit of the Narrator evoking his past, exploring and tracking around the dim room: the camera dollies into – what else? – a mirror: the reflection reveals the 5 year-old Aleksei holding a large glass bottle filled with milk (all covered in what appears to be a single sequence shot; there may be an invisible cut when the camera moves into the mirror. The lighting shifts). There is the distant sound of a dog barking, and a train whistle (a great touch); echoes of childhood.

'Films should be experienced, not explained, thought Andrei Tarkovsky, and no filmmaker surpassed him in being able, as it were, to film the human spirit', commented Neil Sinyard (1992, 158).

There's a nice quote by Federico Fellini in a documentary talking about how impressed the Italian was by Akira Kurosawa's *Rashomon* (1951), a firm favourite with film directors. Somehow, Fellini said, Kurosawa was able to photograph air itself. Fellini was referring to the unsurpassed technique Kurosawa developed of portraying the elements, such as rain and mist (Kurosawa liked to have practical effects such as wind, rain, and fire on hand). It's the same with Tarkovsky (who was deeply influenced by Kurosawa's elemental filmic techniques).

Scene 36. The past (1935-36).

The five year-old boy swimming in a river, in colour, seen from behind, with the camera following him in a boat. The camera tilts up to reveal Maria nearby, washing.

Scene 37. The past (1935-36).

Now we are heading towards the Big Finish.

Inside the *dacha* (in colour), the camera tracks through the living room (which's empty) towards the window. The room looks art directed by the team to look like a still-life painting: a vase of flowers; a dog; some eggs and a book on the window sill.

Outside the *dacha*, in bright sunshine. Birds sing. It is Summer. Seen through the window, the five year-old Aleksei walks out to his sister Marina and grandmother, but the latter is played by the same actress (Maria Tarkovskaya) who plays the aged Maria in the modern-day scenes. She sits in the same pose as the young Maria did in the opening scenes: looking out at the field and forest, and smoking. Aleksei says the lamp is smoking. The past and present are mixed together here.

Scene 38. The present (1974). A Moscow apartment.

In colour, a Doctor (in a white coat, a cameo by co-writer Alexander Misharin)[4] comments on his patient: the patient is the Narrator, seen in the shadows of behind a screen (Andrei Tarkovsky himself played this part, though not his voice, which was by the usual Narrator, Innokenti Smoktunovsky). He is ill in bed. A variety of mirrors line the walls (probably the last few that the designers were able to scavenge – *Mirror* goes thru mirrors like a *Star Wars* movie goes thru plastic lightsabres).

The Doctor tells the people in the room (oddly, a neighbour played by the same actress (Tamara Ogorodnikova) who was the Spanish woman of the earlier Alexander Pushkin reading scene, and an old woman), that people can die of yearning, when their life falls apart. The Narrator's illness in *Mirror*, Tarkovsky

---

[4] Misharin also appears in *Solaris,* playing Shannahan, Berton's expedition host.

said in 1985, 'was necessary in order to convey the author's spiritual crisis, the state of his soul'. And it was a narrative device, so that the Narrator could be recollecting his life.

Ultra-symbolically, the Narrator picks up a tiny bird beside him on the bed. In voiceover, he tells the people in the next room that 'everything will be all right' (and to leave him alone). The Narrator releases the bird into the air in slow motion (the camera moves ahead of him, anticipating his gesture, and the shot moves into slow motion). (Tarkovsky played the dying Narrator himself, and, according to the cinematographer, Georgy Reberg, had wanted to have his face on screen as well as his body. Reberg had persuaded him not to, arguing that it would have made *Mirror* 'uncomfortably, and unacceptably, personal' (JP, 304). Reberg was correct: the director appearing here would be distracting, as if Federico Fellini had popped up in *8 1/2* or *Amarcord* at the end). The hero of *Mirror*, Tarkovsky explained, was fatally selfish and self-absorbed: he was unable to appreciate those around him, incapable of loving them without wanting something in return (ST, 208).

The Narrator dies of guilt – because he can't repay what was given to him as a child. It's a *thematic* ending, but not a *dramatic* one, because it doesn't convince anyone. Let's face it, it's not the most successful portrayal of someone dying of a broken heart in cinema.

But the Narrator doesn't have to die – he's already utterly alone: the movie has portrayed him as a somewhat bitter, misanthropic guy. I do think the visual depiction of the Narrator, including the rather gimmicky, self-conscious idea of not showing his face, is the least successful element in *Mirror*.

Scene 39. The past and present.

The final sequence in the 1975 movie, in colour, which cuts between three time zones. Maria is lying down with the soldier father: this is the oldest image in the film, because Maria is pregnant with her first child, the Narrator (thus the film moves at this point from the Narrator at the end of his life to before the Narrator was born). So it must be about 1930. The man and woman lie in the grass at the edge of the forest, as young lovers, before the house was built.

The second time zone is the present day, when the grandmother (or Maria as an old woman, some 44 years later) visits the childhood home, which is now a ruin. The third time zone is suggested by Maria standing alone in the field, which could indicate the 1942-43 time zone (or it could be 1935-36). There are autobiographical layers to the sequence, because Andrei Tarkovsky's mother is walking in the spot where her house really was, and the children are meant to be her own children, but as they were in 1935/ 36.

The Big Finish of *Mirror* is lit by a beautiful, warm magic hour light, and the action is covered with complex tracking and panning shots.

Shot 1. A slow pan around the landscape surrounding the old house, the Ignatievo Forest. The music is at a low volume: Johann Sebastian Bach's *St John Passion*, the opening passages of strings and clarinets. Tilt and crane down to the couple lying down in the grass.

Shot 2. Aleksei/ Ignat (aged 5) and the old woman are walking in the woodland – this is in the present day (Maria is an old woman revisiting her old house).

Shot 3. C.U. of the ruins of the house, bits of wet wood, a hole full of crockery, in a tracking shot and zoom.

Shot 4. The trees around the *dacha*, but seen now in L.S. from a new perspective: the grandmother walks out of the trees. This is the only time a human being has been seen in this sacred space in *Mirror*, in amongst the trees. It has to be the grandmother who is associated with such a place, the dark forest, because she is (the aged) Maria, the centre of the film and of the Narrator's life, the heart of all the mythopœia. She takes hold of the boy's hand; they survey the smashed house.

Shot 5. Maria deep in thought, perhaps watching the people of the future, perhaps imagining the future, and how she will be in the future – as an old woman and grandmother. The father asks her whether she wants a girl or a boy. This sets her thoughts racing: the actress shows her inner turmoil brilliantly: she cries, bites her lip, sighs, smiles, looks heavenward, then turns, as if to look at:

Shot 6. The grandmother with the boy and girl, walking through the field, away from the ruined house. They walk in the direction of the place where the Doctor was first seen emerging at the beginning of the movie. The music suddenly surges up to full volume. Significantly, Maria is standing in the distance in the field, watching the grandmother and children walking away. Maria has seen into the future, and seen herself returning as an old woman to the smashed house which hasn't yet been built behind her. This is one interpretation. Or it's a curtain call, a final appearance.

Shot 7. A lengthy L.S.: the grandmother and children walk through the fields while the Johann Sebastian Bach choral music carries on playing loudly. The opening movement of Bach's music comes to its abrupt ending; the boy hollers; then he runs and catches up his grandmother; they move away from the camera, which tracks steadily into the wood, receding further and further; it is sunset; the sky is orangey purple; the forest gets darker; the birds at twilight are heard (the camera zooms in towards the end of the shot – reframing, which can seem like an error that would usually be edited out; but it doesn't detract from the beauty of the scene).

A stunning, lyrical ending.

7

CRITICAL RESPONSES TO *MIRROR*

Andrei Tarkovsky's films were often dismissed as élitist puzzles by the Soviet authorities and critics: his works were regarded as movies for minorities. Nikolai Sizov, director of the Moscow Film Studios, said *Mirror* was 'too complex'. For the filmmaker V.N. Naumov, *Mirror* was 'un-understandable' (ibid.). Sergei Gerasimov, the veteran director who was for years chief of the Joint Acting and Directing Workshops at V.G.I.K., where Tarkovsky studied, remarked that Tarkovsky was 'a man of very serious talent' (ibid.).

When Soviet films of the time were expected to be 'social realist', it's understandable why *Mirror* should have seemed so radically different. (Some Russian critics – and movie-makers – couldn't quite accept the idea that Andrei Tarkovsky was making a film about his own life, rather than a larger, social subject).

Michael Dempsey called *Zerkalo* 'intractable', 'ineffable' and 'enigmatic' (1981). 'Enigmatic' *Mirror* certainly is. Some critics said it was 'a crossword puzzle'. Herbert Marshall reckoned in a 1976 article that *Mirror* was very unusual in terms of mid-Seventies Soviet cinema, and was difficult for Soviet critics to understand (95). Nothing like it had been seen in Soviet cinema before, Marshall asserted. *Mirror* is

> not only told entirely subjectively, but from a subjective point of view at different periods of life both in reality and in memories and dreams, from a boy, a teenager, to a man, the director himself, and his father and mother. Such a film has hitherto never been seen on the Soviet screen... here for the

first time is the 'subjective history' of a Soviet filmmaker in his own film. (ib., 95).

According to John Dunlop, *Mirror* 'encountered a wall of opposition on the part of the Soviet film industry'.[5] Some critics (Maya Turoskaya, T. Elmanovits, Mikhail Bakhtin, V.I. Solovyov) saw *Mirror* as the record not of one's person's life, but of a generation. V.I. Solovyov caught the spirit of the movie right when he said in *Novoye russkoye slovo* that *Mirror* seemed to be portraying 'not film images but *my* thoughts, *my* memories' (1989, 11). This occurs from time to time, when viewers regard a movie as so close to their own thinking or experience, it's as if they made the film themselves. Maurice Clavel wrote of *Mirror* that there is 'no other film like it. One can see how little subjectivist this film is. Perhaps it itself is sacrificial, like Russia according to Pushkin'.[6]

Viewers wrote to Andrei Tarkovsky about how much *Mirror* had affected them. Tarkovsky subsequently quoted some of these letters in *Sculpting in Time*. For Leonid Bahktin, part of *Mirror*'s power is precisely its puzzling, mysterious elements. Bahktin wrote:

> As we reach to grab phrases and shots which seem to openly give us the key to the whole, we come to understand that one cannot exhaust the whole, that we must, like the hero, who exists behind the mirror, go over memories, strain our conscience and impressionability over Aleksei's life and our own.[7]

Jacques Grant noted that *Mirror* is not so much an anti-Marxist as an 'a-Marxist' movie; Andrei Tarkovsky avoids confronting politics; Grant saw the motif of the mirror as a barrier, 'placed by the filmmaker between himself and a world which he refuses to see and to discuss' (1978, 68). That's a common criticism among film reviewers, castigating the director for *not* making the film they thought he should have made. Why *should* a personal film about memories of childhood deal with politics or the so-called 'real' world? But of course,

---
5 In A. Lawton, 1992, 241.
6 In J. Passek, 284.
7 L. Batkin, "Ne boyas svovyego golosa", *Iskusstvo Kino*, 11, 1988.

Mirror does address social, historical and political issues throughout, not only by including the many newsreel images, but also evoking a moving scene of Stalinist repression. There are many other movies of childhood which completely avoid references to historical events. In fact, *Mirror* is *very* unusual in being both a film of personal memories *and* wider historical and social issues.

Gilles Deleuze wrote of *Mirror* (in *Cinema*) in terms of the metaphors of crystals, seeds and mirrors: '*Mirror* is a turning crystal', offered Deleuze, which

> turns on itself, like a homing device that searches an opaque environment: what is Russia, what is Russia? The seed seems to be frozen in these sodden, washed and heavily translucent images, with their sometimes bluish, sometimes brown surfaces, while the green environment seems, in the rain, to be unable to go beyond the condition of a liquid crystal which keeps its secret. (1989, 75)

CRITICAL RESPONSE TO ANDREI TARKOVSKY

The critical response to Andrei Tarkovsky's movies has been varied. For some Tarkovsky is a genius, and his films are some of the finest in cinema; for others, his films are pretentious, boring, indulgent, irrelevant and obscure. Jay Leyda, in *Kino,* his magisterial history of Soviet cinema, said that Andrei Tarkovsky learned to bypass the mass audience, making beautiful puzzle films from which 'each flattered spectator could take away his interpretation as the only possible one' (403). Certainly, Tarkovsky flatters his audience, as well as exasperating them. I have said throughout this study that one of the most important aspects of Tarkovsky's films is their openness, enabling the viewer to manœuvre.

Andrei Tarkovsky wanted his movies to be seen and admired: an audience was essential for the artist 'to fulfil his personal spiritual mission', as he grandly put it (ST, 165). Although he did not deliberately try to please his audience (in the Hollywood manner), and hated the commercial pandering to their tastes (ST, 174-5), he also hoped 'fervently that my picture will be accepted and loved' (ST, 170). Of course, that's what most artists want (and especially with something like a feature film, which can soak up years of a filmmaker's life).

For Ivor Montagu, writing in 1973, Andrei Tarkovsky is 'one of the best things to happen in world cinema for a long time'.[8] Giovanni Buttafava called Tarkovsky's movies 'complex heterodox individual works', 'a series of films that turned the ambiguity of everyday life into the subject of severe subtle investigation'.[9] Of Tarkovsky's *œuvre*, Peter Green wrote in 1987: 'this handful of completed works is individually of such weight and vision that each one of them alone might have secured him a place in film history' (1987). Maybe not *Ivan's Childhood*, but any one of Tarkovsky films from *Andrei Roublyov* onwards would guarantee him a place in the cinematic pantheon.

This sentiment was typical of the obituaries British critics wrote, such as Ian Christie and David Robinson. They waxed lyrical about Andrei Tarkovsky. In "Raising the Shroud", Christie noted, though, that 'there is an urgent need now to resist a premature canonisation' (38).

Arthur Aristakisian, a rising star in Russian cinema (he attended V.G.I.K., and his *The Palms* won a Nika for Best Documentary in 1994), was asked if Andrei Tarkovsky had been privileged, in receiving large budgets, and replied '[t]oday it's not a question of money as much as that people have changed. They are corrupt. They find it more and more difficult to think'. Sentiments Tarkovsky would probably agree with.

Up until the mid-1990s, Andrei Tarkovsky was usually given a few lines in histories and encyclopaedias of cinema, but not much more than that.

---

8 Ivor Montagu, 1973, 92. According to Philip French, Ivor Montagu was 'the most extraordinary person ever to review movies'; he was a friend of Eisenstein, had edited Alfred Hitchcock's *The Lodger*, wrote the rules of table tennis, was a producer at Ealing and Gaumont, a lifelong communist, and son of a peer (J. Boorman, 1998, 6).
9 In J. Boorman, 1998, 347.

Tarkovsky was usually placed next to Sergei Paradjanov and his *The Colour of Pomegranates* in movie guides (but being put beside Paradjanov means being in very good company indeed). Usually *Andrei Roublyov* was discussed (it was probably the Tarkovsky film that created the most fuss in the Soviet Union). *Mirror* was the next film cited in the film guides and history books, but the rest of Tarkovsky's cinema was rarely analyzed.

Geoff Andrew wrote in *The Film Handbook* that Andrei Tarkovsky's later movies are 'deeply flawed by self-indulgence [and] tend towards obscurantism and a cold, intellectual aloofness' (280). There is some truth in this: Tarkovsky's films, despite their intense poetry, can seem chilly. But he is not intellectual: he is very anti-intellectual (Tarkovsky wasn't a fan of intellectualized or literary filmmaking, *mise-en-scène* and staging which illustrates an intellectual or literary idea). He makes few concessions to his audience, however. Like Jean-Luc Godard and Carl Theodore Dreyer, he forces the viewer to work – suffer even, but in most cases his artistic rigour is justified.

In another doorstop-sized guidebook to cinema, *The Story of Cinema*, David Shipman admitted he was sent to sleep by Andrei Tarkovsky's films, and left the cinema showing both *Solaris* and *Mirror* before an hour was up. Of *Ivan's Childhood*, Shipman said that its 'exquisite photography... represents nothing but exquisite photography', and the often-used story of a young boy being taught by an older solder 'has never been so unfeelingly projected' (1048). Shipman reacted even more violently to *Mirror*, which he claimed contained no plot, 'nor the slightest resemblance to human behaviour or connection with imaginative thought' (1049); an extraordinary view. For Shipman, Tarkovsky was cultured but not necessarily intelligent enough to make a successful movie.

In the British Film Institute's *Encyclopaedia of European Cinema*, the entry on Andrei Tarkovsky described him as 'a filmmaker's filmmaker'; *Mirror* and *Stalker* were classed as 'two deeply personal and somewhat obscure films, which were partly autobiographical'.[10] Another popular film guidebook, by Leonard Maltin (one of the better American reviewers), was a fan: *Mirror* was 'superbly directed'; *Nostalghia* was 'a provocative, insightful epic, lovingly rendered by one of cinema's true poets'; and *Andrei Roublyov* was a 'magnificent film worthy of comparison with the best of Eisenstein's historical dramas' (L. Maltin, 2000).

In the British 1982 *Sight & Sound* critics' poll, *Andrei Roublyov* was joint tenth (with *2001: A Space Odyssey*); above *Andrei Roublyov* in the poll were the usual celebrated movies: *The General* and *The Searchers* (joint 8th); *Vertigo, The Magnificent Ambersons* and *L'Avventura* (joint 7th); *Battleship Potemkin* (6th), *8 1/2* (5th), *The Seven Samurai* and *Singin' In the Rain* (joint 3rd), *The Rules of the Game* (2nd), with *Citizen Kane* at the top. (But that was Tarkovsky's only appearance in the *Sight & Sound* top ten films). Twenty years later, in 2002, Tarkovsky wasn't on the list of films, or of the top ten film directors. The movie-makers topping the list, polled from movie directors (rather than critics) were Orson Welles, Federico Fellini, Akira Kurosawa, Francis Coppola, Alfred Hitchcock, Stanley Kubrick, Billy Wilder, Ingmar Bergman, Martin Scorsese, David Lean and Jean Renoir). The favourite movies of film directors in the same poll were the usual suspects: *Kane, Godfather, 8 1/2, Lawrence, Strangelove, Bicycle Thieves* and so on).

Film critics and filmmakers did cite Andrei Tarkovsky's movies many times as among their favourite films, but not often enough to put them in the top ten lists, and compete with the *Kanes,* the *Rashomons,* the *Generals* and the *Godfathers*.[11] Film directors such as Oliver Assayas, John Boorman, Vincent Ward, Jonathan Glazer, Gilles Mackinnon,

---

10 G. Vincendeau, 1995, 419.
11 Other critics and filmmakers who put Tarkovsky in their top ten included in the *Sight & Sound* poll Richard Allen, Russell Campbell, Li Cheuk-To, Malgorzata Dipont, Lalitha Gopalan, Peter Hames, Dina Iordanova, Nick James, Kim Ji-Seok, Andrey Plakhov, M.K. Raghavendra, Donald Richie, Philip Strick, Leonard Tsao, Aruna Vasudev, Alexei Balabanov, Roy Andersson, Gore Verbinski, Ann Hui, Clare Law, Lukas Moodysson, Pawel Pawlikowski, and Sanosh Sivan.

Michael Haneke, Scott Hicks, George Sluizer, Jaco van Dormael and Joel Schumacher put a Tarkovsky movie in their list of top ten films. And one or two filmmakers placed Tarkovsky at the top of their lists: Vincent Ward, George Sluizer, Jaco van Dormael, Clare Law, Gilles Mackinnon and Scott Hicks.

Filmographies

MIRROR

Domestic release – Mch 7, 1975. France: 1978. U.S.A.: 1980. GB: 1980.
Length: 106 minutes.
Production company – Mosfilm.

CREW

Director– Andrei Tarkovsky
Aleksandr Misharin – writer
Andrei Tarkovsky – writer
Arseny Tarkovsky – poems
Produced – Erik Waisberg
Original Music – Eduard Artemyev
Cinematography – Georgi Rerberg
Lighting – V. Gusev
Film Editing – Lyudmila Feiginova
Production Design – Nikolai Dvigubsky
Costume Design – Nelli Fomina
Vera Rudina – makeup artist
Maria Chugunova – assistant director
Larissa Tarkovskaya – assistant director
A. Merkulov – set designer
Nikolai Dvigubsky – art director
Semyon Litvinov – sound
Yuri Potapov – special effects
Alexey Nikolaev – camera operator

CAST

Margarita Terekhova – Natalia/ Maroussia – the Mother
Oleg Yankovskiy – the Father
Filipp Yankovsky – Aleksei – 5 years-old
Ignat Daniltsev – Ignat/ Aleksei – 12 years-old
Nikolai Grinko – Print Director
Alla Demidova – Lisa
Yuriy Nazarov – Military trainer
Anatoli Solonitsyn – Forensic doctor
Larissa Tarkovskaya – Nadezha
Tamara Ogorodnikova – Nanny/ Neighbour/ Strange woman at the tea table
Yuri Sventisov – Asafyev
Olga Kizilova – Redhead girl
Tamara Reshetnikova – Secretary
Innokenti Smoktunovsky – Aleksei/ Narrator (voice)
Arseny Tarkovsky – Father (voice)
Aleksandr Misharin – Doctor at the end
Ernesto Del Bosque – a Spaniard
Alejandro Gutiérrez – a Spaniard
Tatiana Del Bosque – a Spaniard
Teresa Del Bosque – a Spaniard
L. Correcer – a Spaniard
Diego García – a Spaniard
Teresa Rames – a Spaniard

Filmography

Andrei Tarkovsky

This is a short filmography of other movies directed by Andrei Tarkovsky: there are other, more detailed filmographies available elsewhere.

There Will be No Leave Today
(Segodnya uvolneniya ne budet)

Short made at VGIK in 1959

The Steamroller and the Violin
(Katok i stripka)

Production company – Mosfilm; script – Andrei Mikhalkov-Konchalovsky and Andrei Tarkovsky; photography – Vadim Yusov in Sovcolour; editor – L. Butuzova; art director – S. Agoyan; music – Vyacheslav Ovchinnikov; sound – V. Krashkovsky
VGIK Diploma project, 1960. Length – 46 minutes
Cast: Sasha – Igor Fomshenko; Sergei – V. Samansky; Girl – Nina Arkhanelskaya; Mother – Marina Adzhubey.

Ivan's Childhood (Ivanovo destvo)

Production company – Mosfilm; script – Mikhail Papava and Vladimir Bogomolov, based on Bogomolov's book *Ivan*; photography – Vadim Yusov in black-and-white; editor – G. Natanson; art director – Evgeni Cherniaev; music – Vyacheslav Ovchinnikov; sound – E. Zelentsova.
Released in 1962. Length – 95 minutes.
Cast: Ivan – Kolya Burlyaev; Captain Kholin – Valentin Zubkov; Lieutenant Galtsev – E. Zharikov; Corporal Katasonych – S. Krylov; Lieutenant-colonel Gryaznov – Nikolai Grinko; Masha – L.Malyavina; Ivan's mother – Irma Tarkovskaya.

Andrei Roublyov

Production company – Mosfilm; producer – Tamara Ogorodnikova; script – Andrei Mikhalkov-Konchalovsky and Andrei Tarkovsky; photography – Vadim Yusov in Scope and black-and-white, part in Sovcolour; editor – Ludmila Feganova; art director – Evgeni Cherniaev; music – Vyacheslav Ovchinnikov; sound – E. Zelentsova.

Production – 1964-66. Domestic release – 1971. U.S.A. release – 1973. Length – 185 minutes. Other versions: 146 minutes, and one 6 minutes longer than the previous longest known, shown in Moscow, 1989.

Cast: Andrei Roublyov – Anatoly Solonitsyn; Krill – Ivan Lapikov; Daniel – Nikolai Grinko; Theophanes the Greek – Nikolai Sergeyev; Mute Girl – Irma Raush Tarkovskaya; Boriska – Nikolai Burlyaev; Buffoon – Rolan Bykov.

Solaris

Production company – Mosfilm; script – Andrei Tarkovsky and Friedrich Gorenstein, based on Stanislaw Lem's book; photography – Vadim Yusov in Scope and Sovcolour; editor – Ludmila Feganova; art director – Mikhail Romadin; music – Eduard Artemiev, J.S. Bach's Chorale Prelude in F minor.

Production – 1969-72. Release – 1972. Length 165 minutes (some versions 144 minutes).

Cast: Chris Kelvin – Donatas Banionis; Hari – Natalia Bondarchuk; Snaut – Yuri Jarvet; Sartorius – Anatoly Solonitsyn; Burton – Vladislav Dvorzhetsky; Kelvin's father – Nikolai Grinko; Gibaryan – Sos Sarkissyan.

Stalker

Production company – Mosfilm; producers – Aleksandra Demidova and Willie Geller; script – Arkady and Boris Strugatsky, based on their story *Roadside Picnic*; photography – Aleksandr Knyazhinsky, colour; lighting supervisor – L. Kazmin; editor – Ludmila Feganova; production designer – Andrei Tarkovsky; music – Eduard Artemiev; sound – V. Sharun.

First screened – 1979. Length – 161 minutes.

Cast: the Stalker – Aleksandr Kaidanovsky; the Writer – Anatoly Solonitsyn; the Scientist – Nikolai Grinko; Stalker's wife – Alisa Freindlikh; Stalker's daughter – Natasha Abramova.

Nostalghia

Production company – Opera Film (Rome)/ RAI Television Rete 2 and Sovinfilm; producers – Manolo Bolognini, Franco Casati, Renzo Rossellini, Daniel Toscan du Plantier; script – Andrei Tarkovsky and Tonino Guerra; photography – Guiseppe Lanci, in Eastman Colour; editor – Erminia Marani, Amedeo Salfa; art director – Andrea Crisanti; sound effects – Massimo Anzellotti, Luciano Anzellotti; sound mixer – Danilo Moroni.

Production, 1981-83. Release – 1983. Length 126 minutes.

Cast: Andrei Gorchakov – Oleg Yankovsky; Domenico – Erland Josephson; Eugenia – Domiziana Giordano; Gorchakov's wife – Patrizia Terreno.

The Sacrifice (Offret)

Production company – Swedish Film Institute (Stockholm)/ Argos Film (Paris), with Film Four International (London), Josephson & Nykvist, Sveriges Television/ SVT 2, Sandrew Film & Teater, with the participation of the French Ministry of Culture; producer – Katinka Farago; script – Andrei Tarkovsky; photography – Sven Nykvist, Eastman Colour and black-and-white; editor – Andrei Tarkovsky and Michal Leszcylowski; art director – Anna Asp; music – J.S. Bach's *St Matthew Passion*, Swedish and Japanese folk music; sound – Owe Svensson, Bosse Persson, Lars Ulander, Christin Lohman, Wille Peterson-Berger.

Release, 1986. Length – 149 minutes.

Cast: Alexander – Erland Josephson; Adelaide – Susan Fleetwood; Otto – Allan Edwall; Julia – Valerie Mairesse; Maria – Gudrun Gísladóttir; Victor – Sven Wollter; Martha – Filippa Franzén; Little Man – Tommy Kjellqvist; Julia – Valerie Mairesse.

Availability

The work of Andrei Tarkovsky is fairly readily available on DVD, video and other formats. There are variations between editions, of course. For instance, the DVD of *Mirror* (from Artificial Eye in the U.K.) contains two different sound mixes (and they are *very* different). In general, the sound mix or dub that was overseen or approved by the filmmakers themselves is the one to go for. And movies are best seen in the original language.

The main distributors of Tarkovsky's works are:
In the U.S.A.: Kino Video. Criterion. Facets.
In Great Britain: Artificial Eye. Criterion. Russico.
In Australia: Shock.

Bibliography

BY ANDREI TARKOVSKY

"Tarkovsky", *Kogda film okonchen* [*When the film is finished*], *Iskusstvo kino*, Moscow, 1964
interview, *Ekran*, 65, Sbornik, Iskusstvo, Moscow, 1966
"Zapechatlennoye vremya [Imprinted time]", *Iskusstvo kino*, 4, 1967
interview, M. Ciment, *Positif*, 109, Oct, 1969
"Vsesoyuznaya pereklichka kinematografistov" [An All-Union Filmmakers' Discussion]", *Iskusstvo kino*, 4, 1971
"Zachem proshloye vstrechayetsya s budushchim? [Why does the past meet the future?]", *Iskusstvo kino*, 11, 1971
Bely, bely den [*Bright, bright day*], Mosfilm, Moscow, 1973
"O Kinobraze [About the film image]", *Iskusstvo kino*, 3, 1979
"My delayem filmy [We make films]", *Kino*, Lithuania, 10, 1981
interview, *Time Out*, 568, Mch, 1981
interview, *Time Out*, 686, Nov, 1981
"Between Two Worlds", interview, *American Film*, Nov, 1983
interview, *Time Out*, 729, Aug, 1984
interview, *The Listener*, Aug, 1984
"A Propos du *Sacrifice*", *Positif*, 303, May, 1986
"Entretien", *Cahiers du Cinéma*, 392, Feb, 1987
"Ya chasto dumayu o vas [I think of you often]", *Iskusstvo kino*, 6, 1987
Le Sacrifice, Schirmer, Munich, 1987
"Strasti po Andreyu [The passion according to Andrei]", interview, *Literaturnoye obozreniye*, 9, 1988
Zerkalo [*Mirror*], Kinostsenarii, 2, Goskino, 1988
"Krasota spasyot mir" ["Beauty will save the world"], *Iskusstvo kino*, 2, 1989
"Vstat na put [Taking the right path]", *Iskusstvo kino*, 2, 1989
Lektsii po kinorezhissure [Lecture on film directing], ed. K. Lopushansky, Lenfilm, Leningrad, 1989
Martyrolog: Tagebücher, 1970-1986, tr. V. Schutz-Bischitzky & M. Milack-Verheyden, Limes, Berlin, 1989
Sculpting in Time: Reflections on the Cinema, tr. K. Hunter-Blair, Faber, London, 1989
Time Within Time: The Diaries, 1970-1986, tr. K. Hunter-Blair, Seagull Books, Calcutta, 1991
Andrei Rublev, tr. K. Hunter-Blair, Faber, London, 1991
Der Spiegel. Filmnovelle, Arbeitstagebücher und Materialien zur Entstehung des Films, Limes Verlag, Berlin, 1993
Collected Screenplays, Faber, London, 1998

Andrei Tarkovski: Récits de jeunesse, Paris, 2004
Diaries, tr. C. Giroldi, ed. P. Rey, Cahiers du cinéma, Paris, 2004
Instant Light: Tarkovsky Polaroids, Thames & Hudson, London, 2004
Interviews, ed. J. Gianvito, University of Mississippi Press, 2006
Bright, Bright Day, Tarkovsky Foundation, 2008
Tarkovsky: Films, Stills, Polaroids and Writings, Thames & Hudson, 2019

OTHERS

N. Abramov. "Dialog s A. Tarkovskim o nauchnoy fantastike na ekrane [Dialogue with A. Tarkovsky about science fiction on the screen]", *Ekran, 1970-1971*, Moscow, 1971

H. Agel. "Andrej Tarkovski", in *Le visage du Christ à l'écran*, Desclée, Paris, 1985

C. Akesson. *The Sacrifice: The Film Companion*, I.B. Tauris, London, 2000

J. Alexander. "Tarkovsky's Last Vision", *Cinema Papers*, Melbourne, May, 1987

R. Altman, ed. *Sound Theory, Sound Practice,* Routledge, London, 1992

Andrej Tarkowskij, Reihe Film, 39, Carl Hanser Verlag, Munich, 1987

G. Andrew. *The Film Handbook*, Longman, London, 1989

L. Anninsky. *Shestidesyatniki i my [The Sixties Generation and We]*, VTPO Kinotsentr, Moscow, 1991

O. Assayas. "Tarkovsky: Seeing is Believing", *Sight & Sound,* Jan, 1997

L. Atwood, ed. *Red Women On the Silver Screen: Soviet Women and Cinema*, Pandora, London, 1993

H. Baba. *The Andrei Tarkovsky Films*, Misuzu Shobou, Tokyo, 2002

L. Bahktin. "Ne boyas svoyego golosa [Unfraid of one's own voice]", *Iskusstvo kino,* 11, 1988

L. Bawden, ed. *The Oxford Companion to Film*, Oxford University Press, Oxford, 1976

A. Bazin. *What is Cinema,* 2 vols, University of California Press, Berkeley, CA, 1960

M. Beja. *Film and Literature: An Introduction,* Longman, London, 1979

R. Bergan & R. Karney. *Bloomsbury Foreign Film Guide*, Bloomsbury, London, 1988

A. Bergesen & A. Greeley. *God In the Movies*, Transaction, 2000

I. Bergman. *Bergman on Bergman, Interviews with Ingmar Bergman,* by S. Björk-man *et al*, tr. P.B. Austin, Touchstone, New York, NY, 1986

—. *Images: My Life In Film,* Faber, London, 1994

R. Bird. *Andrei Rublev*, BFI, London, 2004

—. *Andrei Tarkovsky: Elements of Cinema,* 2008

A. Birkos. *Soviet Cinema*, Archon, Hamden, CT, 1976

E. Blank. "*The Sacrifice*, trapped by its monologues", *Pittsburgh Press*, Jan 2, 1987

J. Boorman, *Projections 8*, Faber, London, 1998

D. Bordwell. "Art cinema as a mode of film practice", *Film Criticism*, 4, 1, 1979

—. *Narration in the Fiction Film*, Routledge, London, 1988

—. *Ozu and the Poetics of Cinema*, British Film Institute, London, 1988

—. & K. Thompson. *Film Art: An Introduction*, McGraw-Hill Publishing Company, New York, NY, 1990

—. *The Cinema of Eisenstein*, Harvard University Press, Cambridge, MA, 1993

F. Borin. *Andrej Tarkovsky*, Venice, 1987

L. Boyadzhieva. *Andrei Tarkovsky*, Glagoslav, 2014

D. Brown. *Soviet Russian Literature Since Stalin*, Cambridge University Press, Cambridge, 1978

S. Bukatman. *Terminal Identity: The Virtual Subject in Postmordern Science Fiction*, Duke University Press, Durham, NC, 1993

G. Buttafava. *Il cinema russo e sovietico*, Torino, 2000

I. Cameron, ed. *The Films of Robert Bresson*, Studio Vista, London, 1969

V. Canby. review of A*ndrei Roublev*, *New York Times*, Oct 10, 1973

P. Cazals. *Sergei Paradjanov*, Cahiers du Cinéma, Paris, 1993

P. Christensen. "Kierkegaardian Motifs in Tarkovsky's *The Sacrifice*", *Soviet and East-European Drama, Theatre and Film*, 7, 2/3, Dec, 1987

I. Christie. "Raising the Shroud", *Monthly Film Bulletin*, Feb, 1987

—. & J. Grafty, eds. *Yakov Protazanov and the Continuity of Russian Cinema*, British Film Institute, London, 1993

—. & R. Taylor, eds. *Eisenstein Rediscovered*, Routledge, London, 1993

— & P. Dodd. *Spellbound: Art and Film*, British Film Institute, London, 1996

—. "Returning to Zero", *Sight & Sound*, Apl, 1998

M. Ciment, ed. *Dossier Positif*, Editions Rivages, Paris, 1988

J. Collins *et al*, eds. *Film Theory Goes to the Movies*, Routledge, New York, NY, 1993

D.A. Cook. *A History of Narrative Film*, W.W. Norton, New York, NY, 1990

J.C. Cooper. *An Illustrated Dictionary of Symbols*, Thames and Hudson, London, 1978

A. Crisanti. "Le décor de *Nostalgia*", in G. Ciment, 1988

A. de Baecque. *Andrei Tarkovski*, Cahiers du Cinéma, Paris, 1989

A. de Jonge. *Stalin and the Shaping of the Soviet Union*, Morrow, New York, NY, 1986

G. Deleuze. *Cinema 1: The Movement Image*, Athlone Press, London, 1989

—. *Cinema 2: The Time Image*, Athlone Press, London, 1989

J. Delmas. "'…comme une fleuve': A*ndrei Roublev*", *Jeune Cinéma*, 42, Dec, 1969

M. Dempsey. "Lost Harmony: Tarkovsky's *The Mirror* and *The*

Stalker", *Film Quarterly,* Autumn, 1981

G. Dolmarovskaya & I. Shilova. *Who's Who in the Soviet Cinema,* Progress, Moscow, 1979

A. Dovzhenko. *Alexander Dovzenko,* MIT Press, Cambridge, MA, 1973

N. Savio D'Sa. "Andrei Rublev: Religious Epiphany in Art", *Journal of Religion and Film,* 3, 2, 1999

Nathan Dunne, Jean-Paul Sartre & Marc Forster. *Tarkovsky,* 2008

Raymond Durgnat. *Films and Feelings,* Faber, London, 1967

A. Dzenis. "The Passion According to Andrei: *Andrei Rublev",* *Metro,* 110, 1997

H. Eagle. *Russian Formalist Film Theory,* University of Michigan Press, Ann Arbor, MI, 1981

A. Easthope, ed. *Contemporary Film Theory,* Longman, London, 1993

J. Elliot. *Eliot's Guide to Films On Video,* Boxtree, London, 1993

T. Elmanovits. *The Mirror of Time: The Films of Andrei Tarkovsky,* Eesti Raamat, Tallinn, 1980

M. Estève, ed. *Etudes Cinématographiques: Andrei Tarkovsky,* 135-138, Lettres Modernes, Paris, 1983

J. Ferguson. *An Illustrated Encyclopaedia of Mysticism,* Thames & Hudson, London, 1976

V.P. Filimonov. *Andrei Tarkovskii: Sny i Iav' o Dome,* 2011

J. Finler. *The Movie Directors Story,* Octopus Books, London, 1985

—. *The Hollywood Story,* Wallflower Press, London, 2003

W. Fisher. "Gorbachev's Cinema", *Sight & Sound,* 56, 4, Autumn, 1987

G.E. Forshey. *American Religious and Biblical Spectaculars,* Praeger, Westport, CT, 1992

N. Galichenko. *Glasnost: Soviet Cinema Responds,* University of Texas Press, Austin, TX, 1991

L.A. Garrett. "Der rätselhafte und geheimnisvolle Andrej Tarkovskij", *Soviet Film,* 7, 1989

—. "Never Be Neutral", *Sight & Sound,* Jan, 1997

—. *Andrei Tarkovsky: a Photographic Chronicle of the Making of the Sacrifice,* 2011

—. *Andrei Tarkovsky,* Glagoslav, 2012

G. Gauthier. *Andrei Tarkovski, Filmo,* 19, Edilig, Paris, 1988

J. Gerstenkorn & S. Strudel. "La quête et la foi", *Études cinématographiques,* 135-8, 1983

A. Gibson. *The Silence of God: Creative Response to the Films of Ingmar Bergman,* Harper & Row, New York, NY, 1969

P. Gibson & R. Gibson, ed. *Dirty Looks: Women, Pornography, Power,* British Film Institute, London, 1993

V. Golovskoy & J. Rimberg. *Behind the Soviet Screen,* Ardis, Ann Arbor, MI, 1986

W. Goodman. "Tarkovsky dies at 54", *New York Times,* Dec 30, 1986

J. Goodwin. *Eisenstein, Cinema and History,* University of Illinois Press, Urbana, IL, 1993

—. ed. *Perspectives On Akira Kurosawa,* G.K. Hall, Boston, MA,

1994

D.J. Goulding, ed. *Post New Wave Cinema in the Soviet Union and Eastern Europe*, Indiana University Press, Bloomington, IN, 1989

—. ed. *Five Filmmakers: Tarkovsky, Forman, Polanski, Szabó, Makavejev*, Indiana University Press, Bloomington, IN, 1994

J. Graffy. "Tarkovsky: The Weight of the World", *Sight & Sound*, Jan, 1997

D. Graham, ed. *Film and Religion*, St Mungo Press, 1997

J. Grant. "Andrei Tarkovsky", *Cinéma*, 231, 1978

P. Green. "The Nostalgia of the Stalker", *Sight and Sound*, Winter, 1984-85

—. "Andrei Tarkovsky", *Sight and Sound*, 56, 2, Spring, 1987

—. *Andrei Tarkovsky: The Winding Quest*, Macmillan, London, 1993

N. Greene. *Pier Paolo Pasolini*, Princeton University Press, Princeton, NJ, 1990

N. Grinko. "Talisman Andreya Tarkovskogo [The talisman of Andrei Tarkovsky]", interview, *Sovetsky ekran*, 2, 1990

L. Halliwell. *Halliwell's Filmgoer's Companion*, 7th edition, Granada, London, 1980

—. *Halliwell's Film Guide*, ed. J. Walker, HarperCollins, London, 1993

—. *Halliwell's Film Guide 2000*, ed. J. Walker, HarperCollins, London, 1999

S. Hancock. "Andrei Tarkovsky: Master of the Cinematic Image", *Mars Hill Review*, 4, 1996

L. Hanlon. *Fragments: Bresson's Film Style*, Farleigh Dickinson University Press, Rutherford, 1986

H. Hart. "The Dialogue of Theology With Film", *Encounter*, 51, 1990

M. Hayward. *Twentieth-century Russian Poetry*, London, 1993

M. Healy. "Cinematography is the major attraction of humorless sermon", *Denver Post*, Feb 20, 1987

M. Heaton. "In films, life, Tarkovsky spurned compromise", *San Francisco Examiner*, Jan 30, 1987

S. Hill. "Soviet Cinema Today", *Film Quarterly*, 20, 4, Summer, 1967

J. Hillier, ed. *Cahiers du Cinéma: The 1950s, New-Realism, Hollywood, New Wave*, Harvard University Press, Cambridge, MA, 1985

—. *The New Hollywood*, Studio Vista, London, 1992

L.C. Hillstrom, ed. *International Dictionary of Films and Filmmakers: Directors*, St James Press, London, 1997

L. Horn. "Tarkovsky's *Sacrifice* charged with images", *Miami Herald*, Nov 21, 1986

A. Horton,& M. Brashinsky. *The Zero Hour: Glasnost and Soviet Cinema in Transition*, Princeton University Press, Princeton, NJ, 1992

—. ed. *Inside Soviet Film Satire*, Cambridge University Press, Cambridge, Cambridge, 1993

—. *Theo Angelopoulos: A Cinema of Contemplation*, Princeton University Press, Princeton, NJ, 1999

T. Hyman. "*Solaris*", *Film Quarterly*, Spring, 1976

E. Hynes. "Stalker", *Reverse Shot*, Spring, 2004

J.J. F. Iaccino. *Jungian Reflections Within the Cinema: A Psychological Analysis of Sci-Fi and Fantasy Archetypes*, Praeger, Westport, CT, 1998

Iskusstvo kino, 2, 1989

W. Jacobsen *et al. Andrej Tarkovsky*, Munich, 1987

V.T. Johnson & G. Petrie. "Andrei Tarkovskii's Films", *Journal of European Studies*, 20, 3, Sept, 1990

—. *The Films of Andrei Tarkovsky. A Visual Fugue*, Indiana University Press, Bloomington, IN, 1994

—. "Tarkovsky", chapter in D. Goulding, 1994

—. "Ethical Exploration" [*Solaris*]", *Sight & Sound*, 2002

Gunnlaugur A. Jonsson & Thorkell A. Ottarsson. *Through the Mirror: Reflections on the Films of Andrei Tarkovsky*, 2006

C.G. Jung. *Memories, Dreams, Reflections*, Collins, London, 1967

W. Kaoru. *St. Tarkovsky*, Japan, 2003

B. Kawin. *Mindscreen: Bergman, Godard and First-Person Film*, Princeton University Press, Princeton, NJ, 1978

—. *How Movies Work*, Macmillan, New York, NY, 1987

V. Kepley. *In the Service of the State: The Cinema of Alexander Dovzenko*, University of Wisconsin Press, Madison, WI, 1986

Kinovedcheskiye zapiski, 9, 1991; 14, 1992

R.P. Kolker. *A Cinema of Loneliness: Penn, Kubrick, Coppola, Scorsese, Altman*, Oxford University Press, New York, NY, 1980

—. *The Altering Eye: Contemporary International Cinema*, Oxford University Press, New York, NY, 1983

—. *A Cinema of Loneliness: Penn, Stone, Kubrick, Scorsese, Spielberg, Altman*, Oxford University Press, New York, NY, 2000

B.A. Kovács & A. Szilágyi. *Les Mondes d'Andrei Tarkovski*, tr. V. Charaire, L'Age d'Homme, Lausanne, 1987

P. Král. "Tarkovsky, or the Burning House", *Screening the Past*, 12, Mch, 2001

J. Kristeva. *Desire in Language: A Semiotic Approach to Literature and Art*, ed. L. Roudiez, tr. T. Gora, *et al*, Blackwell, Oxford, 1982

—. *The Kristeva Reader*, ed. T. Moi, Blackwell, Oxford, 1986

W. La Barre. *The Ghost Dance: The Origins of Religion*, Allen & Unwin, London, 1972

—. *Muelos: A Stone Age Superstition About Sexuality*, Columbia University Press, New York, NY, 1985

J. Lacan. *Ecrits: A Selection*, tr. A. Sheridan, Tavistock Publications, London, 1977

R. Lapsley & M. Westlake, eds. *Film Theory: An Introduction*, Manchester University Press, Manchester, 1988

A. Lawton. *Kinoglasnost: Soviet Cinema in Our Time*, Cambridge University Press, Cambridge, 1992

—. *The Red Screen: Politics, Society, Art in Soviet Cinema*, Routledge, London, 1992

V. Lasareff. *Russian Icons*, Collins, London, 1962

R. Lauder. *God, Death, Art and Love: The Philosophical Vision of*

Ingmar Bergman, Paulist Press, 1989

M. Le Fanu. *Sight & Sound*, Autumn, 1986

—. *The Cinema of Andrei Tarkovsky,* British Film Institute, London, 1987

S. Lem. *Solaris*, Penguin, London, 1981

L. da Vinci. *Selections From the Notebooks,* Oxford University Press, Oxford, 1952

J. Leyda. ed. *Film Makers Speak: Voices of Film Experience,* Da Capo, New York, NY, 1977

—. *Kino: A History of the Russian and Soviet Cinema,* 3rd ed, Allen & Unwin, London, 1983

M. & A. Liehm. *The Most Important Art: Eastern European Film After 1945*, University of California Press, Berkeley, CA, 1977

P. Livington. *Ingmar Bergman and the Rituals of Art,* Cornell University Press, Ithaca, NY, 1982

L. Maltin. ed. *Leonard Maltin's 2001 Movie & Video Guide*, Penguin, London, 2000

E. Marks & I. de Courtivron, eds. *New French feminisms: an anthology,* Harvester Wheatsheaf, Hemel Hempstead, 1981

H. Marshall. "Andrei Tarkovsky's *The Mirror*", *Sight and Sound*, Spring, 1976

—. *Masters of the Soviet Cinema*, Routledge, London, 1983

J.W. Martin & Conrad E. Ostwalt, eds. *Screening the Sacred: Religion, Myth, and Ideology in Popular American Film,* Westview Press, Boulder, CO, 1995

S. Martin. *Andrei Tarkovsky*, Essential Books, London, 2005

T. Martin. *Images and the Imageless: a Study in Religious Consciousness and Film,* Bucknell University Press, 1981

G. Mast *et al,* eds. *Film Theory and Criticism: Introductory Readings*, Oxford Uni-versity Press, New York, NY, 1992

J.R. May & M. Bird, eds. *Religion In Film*, University of Tennessee Press, Knox-ville, TN, 1982

J. Mayne. *Kino and the Woman Question: Feminism and Soviet Silent Film*, Ohio State University Press, OH, 1989

M. McCormick. *Model of a House: An Essay on Andrei Tarkovsky's The Sacrifice*, 2006

L. Menashe. "Glasnost in the Soviet Cinema", *Cineaste*, 16, 1/2, 1988

A. Mengs, *Stalker,* Ediciones Rialp, Spain

C. Metz. *Film Language: A Semiotics of the Cinema,* tr. M. Taylor, Oxford University Press, New York, NY, 1974

D. Miall. "The Self in History: Wordsworth, Tarkovsky and Autobiography", *Wordsworth Circle*, 27, 1996

V.I. Mikhalkovich. *Andrei Tarkovsky*, Znaniye, Moscow, 1989

A. Miller. *Thou Shalt Not Be Aware: Society's Betrayal of the Child,* tr. H. & H. Hannum, Farrar, Straus & Giroux, New York, NY, 1986

J.-A. Miller *et al.* "Dossier on suture", *Screen*, 18, 4, Winter, 1977/ 78

T. Mitchell. "Tarkovsky in Italy", *Sight and Sound,* Winter, 1982-83

—. "Andrei Tarkovsky and *Nostalghia"*, *Film Criticism*, 8, 3, 1984

T. Moi. *Sexual/ Textual Politics: Feminist Literary Theory,*

Methuen, London, 1985
— ed. *French Feminist Thought*, Blackwell, Oxford, 1988
I. Montagu. "Man and Experience: Tarkovsky's World", *Sight and Sound*, Spring, 1973
J. Moore. "Vagabond Desire: Aliens, Alienation and Human Regeneration in Arkday and Boris Strugatsky's *Roadside Picnic* and Andrei Tarkovsky's *Stalker*", in D. Cartmell *et al*, eds., *Alien Identities: Exploring Differences In Film and Fiction*, Pluto Press, London, 1999
J. Nelmes, ed. *An Introduction to Film Studies*, Routledge, London, 1996
Sihusei Nish, *Tarkovsky and His Time. Hidden Truth of Life*, 2011
G. Nowell-Smith, ed. *The Oxford History of World Cinema*, Oxford University Press, Oxford, 1996
S. Nykvist. "Entretien" (with H. Niogret), *Positif*, 324, Feb, 1988
—. & B. Forslund. *In Reverence of Light*, Albert Bonniers Publishing Company, Sweden, 1997
D. Obolensky, ed. *The Penguin Book of Russian Verse*, Penguin, London, 1965
J. Orr & C. Nicholson, eds. *Cinema and Fiction*, Edinburgh University Press, Edinburgh, 1992
—. *Contemporary Cinema*, Edinburgh University Press, Edinburgh, 1998
—. & O. Taxidou, eds. *Postwar Cinema and Modernity: A Film Reader*, Edinburgh University Press, Edinburgh, 2000
J. Panshina. "Rossia v ozhidanii chuda", *Russakaia mysl*, Feb 23, 1978
P.P. Pasolini. *Pasolini on Pasolini*, ed. O. Stack, Thames & Hudson, London, 1969
J.-L. Passek, ed. *Le Cinéma russe*, L'Esquerre, Paris, 1981
A. Pavelin. *Fifty Religious Films*, A.P. Pavelin, Chiselhurst, Kent, 1990
R. Payne. *Leonardo*, Robert Hale, London, 1987
W. Paul. review of *Andrei Roublev*, *Village Voice*, Nov 1, 1973
C. Penley, ed. *Feminism and Film Theory*, Routledge, New York, NY, 1988
—. *et al*, eds. *Close Encounters: Film, Feminism and Science Fiction*, University of Minnesota Press, Minneapolis, MN, 1991
S. Petraglia. *Andrej Tarkovskij*, Edizioni A.I.A.C.E., Turin, 1975
V. Petric, ed. *Film and Dreams: An Approach to Bergman*, Redgrave, South Salem, 1981
—. *Constructivism In Film*, Cambridge University Press, Cambridge, 1987
—. "Tarkovsky's Dream Imagery", *Film Quarterly*, Winter, 1990
G. Petrie & R. Dwyer, eds. *Before the Wall Came Down: Soviet and East European Filmmakers Working in the West*, University Press of America, Lanham, 1990
—. "Andrei Tarkovsky", in G. Nowell-Smith, 1996
L. Yan Pin. "Simvolika Tarkovskogom i daoizma [The symbolism of Tarkovsky and Taoism]", *Kinovedcheskiye zapiski*, 9, 1991
A. Plakhov. "Soviet Cinema in the Nineties", *Sight & Sound*, 58, Spring, 1990
T. Pontara. *Andrei Tarkovsky's Sounding Cinema*, Routledge,

2019

J. Pym. *Film On Four*, British Film Institute, London, 1992

—. ed. *Time Out Film Guide, 1996*, Penguin, London, 1995

D. Quinlan. *The Illustrated Guide to Film Directors*, B.T. Batsford, London, 1983

M. Ratschewa. "The Messianic Power of Pictures: The Films of Andrei Tarkovsky", *Cinéaste*, 13, 1, 1983

D. Richie. *The Films of Akira Kurosawa*, University of California Press, Berkeley, CA, 1965

C. Rickey. "Starkly, a director explores materialism and spirituality", *Philadelphia Inquirer*, Feb 4, 1987

Thomas Redwood. *Andrei Tarkovskys Poetics of Cinema* , 2010

D. Robinson. "Sculptor in Time, Master of Spirit", *The Times*, Jan 3, 1987a

—. "Testament to a Powerful Will", *The Times*, Jan 9, 1987b

A.M. Sandler, ed. *Mir i filmy Andreya Tarkovskogo* [*The World and Films of Andrei Tarkovsky*], Iskusstvo, Moscow, 1991

D. Robinson. *World Cinema*, Methuen, London, 1981

—. "Sculptor in Time, Master of Spirit", *The Times*, Jan 3, 1987a

—. "Testament to a Powerful Will", *The Times*, Jan 9, 1987b

W.H. Rockett. *Devouring Whirlwind: Terror and Transcendence in the Cinema of Cruelty*, Greenwood Press, New York, NY, 1988

S. Rohdie. *Antonioni*, British Film Institute, London, 1990

—. *The Passion of Pier Paolo. Pasolini*, British Film Institute, London, 1995

J. Romney. "Future Soul [*Solaris*]", *Sight & Sound*, 2002

J. Rosenbaum. "Inner Space: Exploring Tarkovsky's *Solaris*", *Film Comment*, 26, 4, Aug, 1990

B.G. Rosenthal, ed. *The Occult in Russian & Soviet Culture*, Cornell University Press, Ithaca, NY, 1997

R. Ruiz. *The Poetics of Cinema*, Dis Voir, Paris, 1995

T. Sabulis. "Director's final *Sacrifice* truly a gift", *Dallas Times Herald*, Jan 16, 1987

D. Salynsky. "Rezhissyor i mif [Director and myth]", *Iskusstvo kino*, 12, 1989

A.M. Sandler, ed. *Mir i filmy Andreya Tarkovskogo* [*The World and Films of Andrei Tarkovsky*], Iskusstvo, Moscow, 1991

J. Sanford. *The New German Cinema*, Da Capo Press, New York, NY, 1982

J.P. Sartre. *Situations VII*, Gallimard, Paris, 1965

D. Shipman. *The Story of Cinema*, Hodder & Stoughton, London, 1984

P. Shrader. *Transcendental Style In Film: Ozu, Bresson, Dreyer*, Da Capo Press, 1972

E. Siciliano. *Pasolini*, Random House, New York, NY, 1982

L. Sider *et al*, eds. *Soundscapes: The School of Sound Lectures 1998-2001*, Wall-flower Press, London, 2003

N. Sinyard. *Children in the Movies*, Batsford, London, 1992

P. Adams Sitney, ed. *The Film Culture Reader*, Praeger, New York, NY, 1970

—. ed. *The Avant-Garde Film: A Reader of Theory and Criticism*, New York University Press, New York, NY, 1978

—. *Visionary Film: The American Avant-Garde, 1943-1978,* 2nd ed., Oxford University Press, New York, NY, 1979
—. *Vital Crises in Italian Cinema,* University of Texas Press, Austin, TX, 1995
Nariman Skakov. *The Cinema of Tarkovsky: Labyrinths of Space and Time (Kino: the Russian and Soviet Cinema),* 2012
T. Slater. *Handbook of Soviet and East European Films and Filmmakers,* Greenwood, Westport, CT, 1992
V. Solovyov. "Semeynaya khronika ottsa i syna Tarkovskikh [The family chronicle of Tarkovsky's father and son]", *Novoye russkoye slovo,* 12 May, 1989
A. Stanbrook. "The Return of Paradjanov", *Sight & Sound,* 55, 4, Autumn, 1986
V.I. Stoichita. *Leonardo da Vinci,* Abbey Library, London, 1978
P. Strick. *"The Sacrifice", Monthly Film Bulletin,* Jan, 1987
—. "Tarkovsky's Lost Minutes", *The Times,* July 12, 1989
—. "Releasing the Balloon, Raising the Bell", *Monthly Film Bulletin,* Feb, 1991
A. & B. Strugatsky. *Roadside Picnic,* Pocket Books, New York, NY, 1978
O. Surkova. "Avtobiograficheskiye motivy v tvorchestve Andreya Tarkovskogo [Autobiographic motifs in the creative work of Andrei Tarkovsky]", *Kino-vedcheskiye zapiski,* Moscow, 9, 1991
—. *Tarkovsky and I,* Zebra E, Dekont, 2002
D. Suvin. "Arkady and Boris Strugatsky", in J. Clute & P. Nicholls, eds. *The Encyclopaedia of Science Fiction,* Orbit, London, 1993
O. Svensson. "On Tarkovsky's *The Sacrifice*", in L. Sider, 2003
N. Synessios. *Mirror,* I.B. Tauris, London, 2001
P. Taggart. "Weighty Film", *Austin American-Statesman,* April 3, 1987
M. Tarkovskaya, ed. *O Tarkovskom* [*About Tarkovsky*], Progress Publishers, Moscow, 1989
Arseny Tarkovsky. *Stikhotvoreniya* [*Poems*], Khudozhestvennaya literatura, Moscow, 1974
—. *Poems,* Greville Press Poetry, 1992
—. *Blagoslovennyi svet,* St Petersburg, 1993
—. *Sobranie sochinenii* [*Collected Works*], 3 vols, Moscow, 1991-93
—. *Life, Life: Selected Poems,* tr. V. Rounding, Crescent Moon, 1999/ 2008
R. Taylor & I. Christie, eds. *The Film Factory: Russian and Soviet Cinema in Documents,* Routledge, London, 1988
—. *Inside the Film Factory: New Approaches to Russian and Soviet Cinema,* Routledge, London, 1991
—. & D. Spring, eds. *Stalinism and Soviet Cinema,* Routledge, London, 1993
—. *et al,* eds. *The BFI Companion to Eastern European and Russian Cinema,* British Film Institute, London, 2000
V. Terras, ed. *Handbook to Russian Literature,* New Haven, CT, 1985
K. Thompson & D. Bordwell. *Film History: An Introduction,*

McGraw-Hill, New York, NY, 1994
- D. Thomson. *A Biographical Dictionary of the Cinema*, Secker & Warburg, London, 1978
- E. Törnqvist. *Between Stage and Screen: Ingmar Bergman Directs*, Amsterdam University Press, Amsterdam, 1995
- A. Truppin. "And Then There Was Sound: The Films of Andrei Tarkovsky", in R. Altman, 1992
- M. Turovskaya. *Tarkovsky: Cinema as Poetry,* tr. N. Ward, ed. I. Christie, Faber, London, 1989
- P. Usai *et al*, eds. *Silent Witnesses: Russian Films 1908-1919*, British Film Institute, London, 1989
- *Variety*. "*Sacrifice* Rolls in Sweden Next May", *Weekly Variety*, Sept 12, 1984
- Laura Vermon. *A Closer Look Into the Life and Famous Works of Andrei Tarkovsky*, 2012
- J. Verniere. "A beautiful *Sacrifice"*, *Boston Herald*, Nov 7, 1986
- D. Vertov. *Kino Eye*, ed. A. Michelson, University of California Press, Berkeley, CA, 1984
- G. Vincendeau, ed. *Encyclopaedia of European Cinema*, British Film Institute, London, 1995
- T. Vinokuroya. "Khozhdeniye po mukam *Andreya Rublyova* [The tormented path of *Andrei Rublyov*]", *Iskusstvo kino*, 10, 1989
- Y. Vorontsov & I. Rachuk. *The Phenomenon of Soviet Cinema*, Progress, Moscow, 1980
- J. Vronskaya. *Young Soviet Film Makers,* Allen & Unwin, London, 1972
- G. Watkins. "Seeing and Being Seen: Distinctively Filmic and Religious Elements in Film", *Journal of Religion and Film,* 3, 2, 1999
- E. Weiss & J. Belton. *Film Sound: Theory and Practice,* Columbia University Press, New York, NY, 1989
- D. Wilson, ed. *Sight and Sound: A Fiftieth Anniversary Selection,* Faber, London, 1982
- R. Wood. *Ingmar Bergman*, Praeger, New York, NY, 1969
- F. Yermash. "On byl khudozhnik [He was an artist]", *Sovetskaya kultura*, Sept 9, 1989 & Sept 12, 1989
- V. Young. *Cinema Borealis: Ingmar Bergman and the Swedish Ethos,* Avon, New York, NY, 1971
- D. Youngblood. "Post-Utopian History as Art and Politics: Andrei Tarkovsky's *Andrei Roublev*", in V. Sobchack, 1995
- R.C. Zaehner. *Mysticism, Sacred and Profane*, Oxford University Press, Oxford, 1957
- M. Zak. *Andrei Tarkovsky: Tvorchesky portret* [*Andrei Tarkovsky: an artistic portrait*], Soyuzinformkino, Moscow, 1988
- N. Zorkaya. "Zametki k portretu Andreya Tarkovskogo [Remarks towards a portrait of Andrei Tarkovsky]", *Kino panorama*, 2, 1977
- —. *The Illustrated History of the Soviet Cinema*, Hippocrene Books, New York, NY, 1990

JEREMY ROBINSON has published poetry, fiction, and studies of J.R.R. Tolkien, Samuel Beckett, Thomas Hardy, André Gide and D.H. Lawrence. Robinson has edited poetry books by Novalis, Ursula Le Guin, Friedrich Hölderlin, Francesco Petrarch, Dante Alighieri, Arseny Tarkovsky, and Rainer Maria Rilke.

Books on film and animation include: *The Akira Book* • *The Art of Katsuhiro Otomo* • *The Art of Masamune Shirow* • *The Ghost In the Shell Book* • *Fullmetal Alchemist* • *Cowboy Bebop: The Anime and Movie* • *The Cinema of Hayao Miyazaki* • *Hayao Miyazaki: Pocket Guide* • *Princess Mononoke: Pocket Movie Guide* • *Spirited Away: Pocket Movie Guide* • *Blade Runner and the Cinema of Philip K. Dick* • *Blade Runner: Pocket Movie Guide* • *The Cinema of Donald Cammell* • *Performance: Donald Cammell: Nic Roeg: Pocket Movie Guide* • *Pasolini: Il Cinema di Poesia/ The Cinema of Poetry* • *Salo: Pocket Movie Guide* • *The Trilogy of Life Movies: Pocket Movie Guide* • *The Gospel According To Matthew: Pocket Movie Guide* • *The Ecstatic Cinema of Tony Ching Siu-tung* • *Tsui Hark: The Dragon Master of Chinese Cinema* • *The Swordsman: Pocket Movie Guide* • *A Chinese Ghost Story: Pocket Movie Guide* • *Ken Russell: England's Great Visionary Film Director and Music Lover* • *Tommy: Ken Russell: The Who: Pocket Movie Guide* • *Women In Love: Ken Russell: D.H. Lawrence: Pocket Movie Guide* • *The Devils: Ken Russell: Pocket Movie Guide* • *Walerian Borowczyk: Cinema of Erotic Dreams* • *The Beast: Pocket Movie Guide* • *The Lord of the Rings Movies* • *The Fellowship of the Ring: Pocket Movie Guide* • *The Two Towers: Pocket Movie Guide* • *The Return of the King: Pocket Movie Guide* • *Jean-Luc Godard: The Passion of Cinema* • *The Sacred Cinema of Andrei Tarkovsky* • *Andrei Tarkovsky: Pocket Guide.*

'It's amazing for me to see my work treated with such passion and respect. There is nothing resembling it in the U.S. in relation to my work.'
(Andrea Dworkin)

'This model monograph – it is an exemplary job, and I'm very proud that he has accorded me a couple of mentions… The subject matter of his book is beautifully organised and dead on beam.'
(Lawrence Durrell, on *The Light Eternal: A Study of J.M.W. Turner*)

'Jeremy Robinson's poetry is certainly jammed with ideas, and I find it very interesting for that reason. It's certainly a strong imprint of his personality.'
(Colin Wilson)

'*Sex-Magic-Poetry-Cornwall* is a very rich essay... It is a very good piece… vastly stimulating and insightful.'
(Peter Redgrove)

ARTS, PAINTING, SCULPTURE

web: www.crmoon.com • e-mail: cresmopub@yahoo.co.uk

The Art of Andy Goldsworthy
Andy Goldsworthy: Touching Nature
Andy Goldsworthy in Close-Up
Andy Goldsworthy: Pocket Guide
Andy Goldsworthy In America
Land Art: A Complete Guide
The Art of Richard Long
Richard Long: Pocket Guide
Land Art In Great Britain
Land Art in Close-Up
Land Art In the U.S.A.
Land Art: Pocket Guide
Installation Art in Close-Up
Minimal Art and Artists In the 1960s and After
Colourfield Painting
Land Art DVD, TV documentary
Andy Goldsworthy DVD, TV documentary

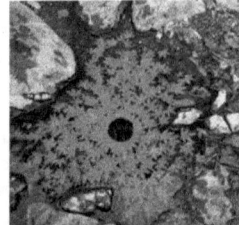

The Erotic Object: Sexuality in Sculpture From Prehistory to the Present Day
Sex in Art: Pornography and Pleasure in Painting and Sculpture
Postwar Art
Sacred Gardens: The Garden in Myth, Religion and Art
Glorification: Religious Abstraction in Renaissance and 20th Century Art
Early Netherlandish Painting
Jasper Johns
Brice MardenLeonardo da Vinci
Piero della Francesca
Giovanni Bellini
Fra Angelico: Art and Religion in the Renaissance
Mark Rothko: The Art of Transcendence
Frank Stella: American Abstract Artist
Alison Wilding: The Embrace of Sculpture
Vincent van Gogh: Visionary Landscapes
Eric Gill: Nuptials of God
Constantin Brancusi: Sculpting the Essence of Things
Max Beckmann
Gustave Moreau
Caravaggio
Egon Schiele: Sex and Death In Purple Stockings
Delizioso Fotografico Fervore: Works In Process 1
Sacro Cuore: Works In Process 2
The Light Eternal: J.M.W. Turner
The Madonna Glorified: Karen Arthurs

LITERATURE

J.R.R. Tolkien: The Books, The Films, The Whole Cultural Phenomenon
J.R.R. Tolkien: Pocket Guide
Beauties, Beasts and Enchantment: Classic French Fairy Tales
Tolkien's Heroic Quest
Brothers Grimm: German Popular Stories
Sexing Hardy: Thomas Hardy and Feminism
Thomas Hardy's *Tess of the d'Urbervilles*
Thomas Hardy's *Jude the Obscure*
Thomas Hardy: The Tragic Novels
Love and Tragedy: Thomas Hardy
The Poetry of Landscape in Hardy
Wessex Revisited: Thomas Hardy and John Cowper Powys
Wolfgang Iser: Essays and Interviews
Petrarch, Dante and the Troubadours
Maurice Sendak and the Art of Children's Book Illustration
Andrea Dworkin

Cixous, Irigaray, Kristeva: The *Jouissance* of French Feminism
Julia Kristeva: Art, Love, Melancholy, Philosophy, Semiotics and Psychoanalysis
Hélene Cixous I Love You: The *Jouissance* of Writing
Luce Irigaray: Lips, Kissing, and the Politics of Sexual Difference
Peter Redgrove: Here Comes the Flood
Peter Redgrove: Sex-Magic-Poetry-Cornwall
Lawrence Durrell: Between Love and Death, East and West
Love, Culture & Poetry: Lawrence Durrell
Cavafy: Anatomy of a Soul
German Romantic Poetry: Goethe, Novalis, Heine, Hölderlin
Novalis: *Hymns To the Night*
Feminism and Shakespeare
Shakespeare: *The Sonnets*
Shakespeare: Love, Poetry & Magic
The Passion of D.H. Lawrence
D.H. Lawrence: Symbolic Landscapes
D.H. Lawrence: Infinite Sensual Violence
The Ecstasies of John Cowper Powys

Sensualism and Mythology: The Wessex Novels of John Cowper Powys
Amorous Life: John Cowper Powys (H.W. Fawkner)
Postmodern Powys: New Essays on John Cowper Powys (Joe Boulter)
Rethinking Powys: Critical Essays on John Cowper Powys
Paul Bowles & Bernardo Bertolucci
Rainer Maria Rilke
Joseph Conrad: *Heart of Darkness*
In the Dim Void: Samuel Beckett
Samuel Beckett Goes into the Silence
André Gide: Fiction and Fervour
Jackie Collins and the Blockbuster Novel
Blinded By Her Light: The Love-Poetry of Robert Graves

POETRY

Ursula Le Guin: *Walking In Cornwall*
Peter Redgrove: Here Comes The Flood
Peter Redgrove: Sex-Magic-Poetry-Cornwall
Dante: Selections From the *Vita Nuova*
Petrarch, Dante and the Troubadours
William Shakespeare: *The Sonnets*
William Shakespeare: Complete Poems
Blinded By Her Light: The Love-Poetry of Robert Graves
Emily Dickinson: Selected Poems
Emily Brontë: Poems
Thomas Hardy: Selected Poems
Percy Bysshe Shelley: Poems
John Keats: Selected Poems
John Keats: Poems of 1820
D.H. Lawrence: Selected Poems
Edmund Spenser: Poems
Edmund Spenser: *Amoretti*
John Donne: Poems
Henry Vaughan: Poems
Sir Thomas Wyatt: Poems
Robert Herrick: Selected Poems
Rilke: Space, Essence and Angels in the Poetry of Rainer Maria Rilke
Rainer Maria Rilke: Selected Poems
Friedrich Hölderlin: Selected Poems
Arseny Tarkovsky: Selected Poems
Paul Verlaine: Selected Poems
Novalis: *Hymns To the Night*
Arthur Rimbaud: Selected Poems
Arthur Rimbaud: *A Season in Hell*
Arthur Rimbaud and the Magic of Poetry
D.J. Enright: By-Blows
Jeremy Reed: *Brigitte's Blue Heart*
Jeremy Reed: *Claudia Schiffer's Red Shoes*
Gorgeous Little Orpheus
Radiance: New Poems
Crescent Moon Book of Nature Poetry
Crescent Moon Book of Love Poetry
Crescent Moon Book of Mystical Poetry
Crescent Moon Book of Elizabethan Love Poetry
Crescent Moon Book of Metaphysical Poetry
Crescent Moon Book of Romantic Poetry
Pagan America: New American Poetry

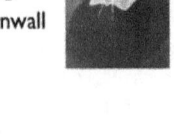

MEDIA, CINEMA, FEMINISM and CULTURAL STUDIES

J.R.R. Tolkien: The Books, The Films, The Whole Cultural Phenomenon
J.R.R. Tolkien: Pocket Guide
The *Lord of the Rings* Movies: Pocket Guide
The Ghost Dance: The Origins of Religion
The Cinema of Hayao Miyazaki
Hayao Miyazaki: *Princess Mononoke*: Pocket Movie Guide
Hayao Miyazaki: *Spirited Away*: Pocket Movie Guide
The Peyote Cult
HomeGround: The Kate Bush Anthology
Tim Burton : Hallowe'en For Hollywood
Ken Russell
Cixous, Irigaray, Kristeva: The *Jouissance* of French Feminism
Julia Kristeva: Art, Love, Melancholy, Philosophy, Semiotics and Psychoanalysis
Luce Irigaray: Lips, Kissing, and the Politics of Sexual Difference
Hélene Cixous I Love You: The *Jouissance* of Writing
Andrea Dworkin
'Cosmo Woman': The World of Women's Magazines
Women in Pop Music
Discovering the Goddess (Geoffrey Ashe)
The Poetry of Cinema
The Sacred Cinema of Andrei Tarkovsky
Andrei Tarkovsky: Pocket Guide
Andrei Tarkovsky: *Mirror*: Pocket Movie Guide
Walerian Borowczyk: Cinema of Erotic Dreams
Jean-Luc Godard: The Passion of Cinema
Jean-Luc Godard: Pocket Guide
John Hughes and Eighties Cinema
Ferris Buller's Day Off: Pocket Movie Guide
The Cinema of Richard Linklater
Liv Tyler: Star In Ascendance
Blade Runner and the Films of Philip K. Dick
Paul Bowles and Bernardo Bertolucci
Media Hell: Radio, TV and the Press
Detonation Britain: Nuclear War in the UK
Feminism and Shakespeare
Wild Zones: Pornography, Art and Feminism
Sex in Art: Pornography and Pleasure in Painting and Sculpture
Sexing Hardy: Thomas Hardy and Feminism

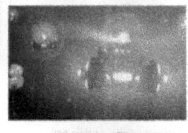

The Light Eternal is a model monograph, an exemplary job. The subject matter of the book is beautifully organised and dead on beam. (Lawrence Durrell)
It is amazing for me to see my work treated with such passion and respect. (Andrea Dworkin)
Sex-Magic-Poetry-Cornwall is a very rich essay... It is like a brightly-lighted box. (Peter Redgrove)

CRESCENT MOON PUBLISHING P.O. Box 1312, Maidstone, Kent, ME14 5XU, Great Britain
0044-1622-729593   cresmopub@yahoo.co.uk   www.crmoon.com

www.ingramcontent.com/pod-product-compliance
Lightning Source LLC
Chambersburg PA
CBHW060536100426
42743CB00009B/1544